Sky Stories 2
From Jodels to Jets

Dave Unwin

First Published by Pigs Might Fly
Publishing 2022

Pigs Might Fly Publishing

www.pigsmightflypublishing.com
ISBN 9798368018140

Contents

Thanks

If you're surprised to be reading Sky Stories 2, how do you think I feel! The original was produced while I was recovering from my Sea Fury crash, and was intended primarily for my mum & dad. However, it sold so well and I got so many nice emails and letters asking me when I'd produce another anthology that it would've been rude not to.

Of course, all the flight tests contained in this book were far from solo efforts, so I'd like to thank everyone who either let me fly their aircraft, flew the cameraship or simply made it happen. So, I must thank (in no particular order) Tom Moloney, Peter Holloway, Art Mearns, Thom Richard, Eskil Amdal, Peter Kosogorin, Jim Harley, Pete Brand, Richard 'Tricky' Ellingworth, DJ Gibbs, Torquil Norman, Henry Labouchere, Philip Whiteman, Martin Willing, Roger Pitman, Jeremy and Oliver Taylor, Mark Murphy, Bob Grimstead, Jean Munn, Sammy Purcell, Keith Richards, Bob Morcom, Jerome Zbinden, Martin 'Canyon' Mendel and Alan Munro (AKA 'Salt One').

Special thanks to Tony Spencer for helping me keep my Jodel D.9 Buzz going.

I must also thank my wife Lizzie for superlative sub-editing skills and my sons Will and George for abuse and encouragement.

Profound thanks must also go to Darren Harbar, Jim Lawrence, and especially Keith Wilson, for letting me use some of their amazing images.

Extra special thanks are due to Mike Carr of Carr Creative for turning those amazing images into pencil sketches and designing the superb cover.

Finally, I'd like to thank you, the reader. I had a lot of fun flying the aircraft contained in this anthology, and I sincerely hope you enjoy reading about them as much as I enjoyed flying them.

Chapter 1
Race Against Time

"This is my last call, I'm going into the field now!"
Back at base, as Gary's final transmission faded away, the CFI turned to study the map of the Brecon Beacons. "Dave, get ready to launch," said Gerry, still scrutinising the map. "We'll have to find him quickly as that's pretty sparsely-populated country. I'll see if anyone airborne can call him. I wish he'd taken his phone." Even as Gerry turned to the radio, I was moving towards the door to see if I could borrow a hand-held transceiver. The Pawnee's radio had gone U/S the previous day and I was already thinking hard about the forthcoming field retrieve, my first. A radio could well prove to be very useful as Gary

would both see and hear me long before I'd see him. Upon re-entering the clubhouse with my newly-procured radio I was immediately aware that the initial air of tension had eased. "He's down and in good shape," reported a relieved Gerry. "Alistair's been talking to him. He says he's not exactly sure where he is but he thinks its aerotowable. Alistair's in the Beacons in his Vega, if he can get high enough he's going to try to have a look around on the way back". Gerry indicated an area on the map and said, "I think he's probably somewhere around Sennybridge, Dave, so get going."

I climbed into the Pawnee's cockpit and rapidly fastened my harness, pleased that Gary was down in one piece (it was his first field landing) and thankful that we had regained contact with him. As the four-bladed propeller blurred into noisy life, I reflected briefly on the 'star' of this rapidly unfolding drama. Sailplanes land out hundreds of times a year, and although the accident rate is high (one out-landing in 40 results in some kind of damage), it is nevertheless not an extraordinary event. What was different about this one was the pilot; Gary Bennett was a paraplegic.

That morning Gerry had declared that it was a perfect day to visit the spectacular ruins of Cerreg Cennen Castle and that he would be going there in his K-6. Gary eagerly accepted the chance of a lead-and-follow through the mountains, especially as the leader would be flying a similar ship to his own. They had made good time to the lonely crag of Cerreg Cennen and the ruins of its fairy tale fortress, but had become separated on the way back. Now Gary was alone and down somewhere.

Pre-flight checks completed, I smoothly opened the throttle to full power and the lightly-loaded Pawnee leapt up into the summer sky. With the cowling aimed due west, we climbed swiftly and steadily, occasionally weaving the long nose from side to side while scanning for traffic. At one point I saw the Vega sliding swiftly homeward. The sailplane looked very low and the day was dying; I hoped Alistair hadn't compromised himself while searching for the K-6.

Soon I was rapidly approaching the area where we believed Gary had gone down, and I began to bring the power back slowly while pulling the carb heat to 'on' and adjusting the trim. As I fumbled with the radio, I scanned each field worriedly, hoping to catch a glimpse of the glider. Although this was to be my first field retrieve, I was confident that I could land in any reasonable field and, if at all possible, tow Gary out. But what if I simply couldn't find him? As far as I knew Gary was still alone and obviously unable to leave his cockpit unaided. There would be daylight for several hours yet, but my aircraft's prodigious thirst would see me 'tanks dry' long before sunset; I had to find him soon or he might be facing a long and uncomfortable night.

Having removed my headset I turned the volume on the transceiver to 'high', clamped it to my ear and bellowed into it (believe me, the cockpit of a

Pawnee is a noisy place). "Kilo Six, Kilo Six, this is Papa Alpha. Where are you, Gary?" The instantaneous reply was startlingly clear and strong. "Papa Alpha, Papa Alpha, I'm in the field right in front of you, right in front of you!" I weaved the long nose slightly to one side and it all clicked into focus. The little K-6 was quite difficult to see, even though it was in the actual field which, by great good fortune, I was flying straight at.

As I began to circle down, my initial impression was that the field seemed ideal, being much longer than the main runway at Talgarth and considerably flatter. The grass surface appeared reasonably short and the landing run was straight into wind. Spiralling lower, I saw a small group of people had started to push the glider backwards and several cars were parked by the field. I also took note of the trees bordering the upwind boundary. After a quick shout to Talgarth base, I stowed the radio, made a low pass to inspect the field more closely and then rolled the Pawnee gently onto the grass.

"No problem" I thought to myself, although the trees upwind looked taller now that I was on the ground.

Even by the time I'd taxied back to the waiting sailplane, the number of people standing by the K-6 had grown and as I began to climb down from the cockpit, another car was pulling up by the field. We were causing quite a stir! Obviously, the arrival of an aircraft without an engine, flown by a man who couldn't walk, was a rare sight in these parts.

I found Gary sitting on the ground by the nose of his sailplane and grinning from ear to ear. He delightedly informed me of the locals' horror when they'd initially discovered that he couldn't walk. Apparently, some people had seen him land near Crai village, were puzzled when he didn't get out of the cockpit and had investigated. Upon learning that he'd been unable to walk before he'd set off, their horror had turned to amazement. Gary had spent the rest of the afternoon explaining to the ever-growing crowd about the clever engineering that enabled him to fly the aircraft, the fact that he was on his way back to Talgarth from Cerreg Cennen and that, no, the propeller hadn't dropped off.

While Gary was being lifted into his cockpit by a pair of burly farmhands, I found and thanked the farmer whose field it was, then showed his interested sons the Pawnee's controls while assuring them that no, Gary really hadn't had a propeller when he'd set off. With all those courtesies attended to, I shook hands with half the population of Crai and noted that the trees now seemed even bigger.

Having briefed a farmhand how to hold the glider's wing, I hooked the tow rope on and, feeling a bit like an old-time barnstormer, gave the by-now quite sizeable crowd a final wave and climbed back into the cockpit. The motor started eagerly and, with checks completed and the slack taken up, I stood on the brakes, ran the engine up to full power and accelerated away down the field towards the waiting trees. The combination lifted off quite quickly and I held the tug in ground effect until the needle of the ASI swung through 70kt, and then rotated into a steep climb. For a second the treetops almost seemed to be reaching up to grasp the Pawnee, then we were soaring above them and I exhaled, set climb power and headed for the Black Mountains and home.

And what did I learn about flying from that? Well, that a single crew low-winged monoplane makes a pretty poor search aircraft, that even a hand-held is better than no radio at all, and that although it may be quite easy to land in a field, it might be a lot trickier to get back out.

Oh, and that you don't have to be able to walk, to be able to fly.

Chapter 2
BAC Strikemaster

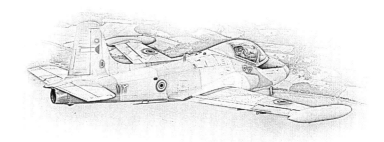

I smoothly open the throttle to 85% rpm against the brakes, release them, and as the jet bounds forward increase power to 100%. With the wind straight down the runway the jet tracks straight and true as the airspeed builds. The ASI's needle and the rudder come alive at roughly the same speed as the Strikemaster surges down Duxford's runway. Now the needle is moving faster than the second hand of a watch as the centreline blurs into a continuous white stripe. As the speed hits 90kt I ease the stick back and wait a second. After a momentary pause, the nosewheel lifts off, followed swiftly at about 105kt by the mains. The bumping, jolting sensation stops instantly, as our clumsy wheeled vehicle miraculously transforms itself into a lithe, vital creature of the air.

I've always liked tough, functional flying machines, and even on the ground the Strikemaster looks sturdy and practical, right down to the rugged-looking wide track undercarriage. G-UNNY is a Mk.87, one of six delivered to the Kenyan air force in 1970 and is owned by Transair boss Tom Moloney, and as he shows me around the aircraft I am extremely impressed with its rugged construction, and its overall condition. The engine - a Rolls-Royce Viper 535 turbojet – is a thirsty beast, particularly when operated at low altitude, and even though the numerous internal fuel tanks have a total capacity of 1,227 litres, they are invariably supplemented by the tip-tanks which carry 436 litres. Access to the cockpit is by climbing up from the back of the wing via walkways on the wings and on top of the air intakes. I pause by the cockpit sill and view the Martin-Baker Mk.4 ejection seat with mixed feelings. Unlike later rocket-propelled seats, these use three cartridges and gives you everything it's got in the first tenth of a second. It's a fully-automatic seat – all I must do is pull either of the ominous-looking black-and-yellow handles. If we need to eject, the seat will probably save my life. However, my middle-aged spine is unlikely to enjoy a vertical acceleration of 80 feet/second!

Having settled onto the right-hand seat, I begin the complex process of strapping in. Along with the leads and hoses for the helmet and oxygen mask, there are leg restraints, a lanyard for the integral seat dinghy and the combined seat/parachute harness to connect. Tom has hundreds of hours on type and makes strapping in look easy. It's not.

Finally strapped in, I familiarise myself with the controls and instruments. The cockpit is typical of a military jet of this vintage, and initially looks quite cluttered and confusing. There are knobs, buttons, levers and handles everywhere, plus myriad toggle switches. The basic 'six pack' of flight instruments follow the traditional RAF arrangement, and are in the centre of the panel, surrounded by a white line to delineate them from the other dials. The Jet Pipe Temperature, rpm, hydraulic pressure and fuel gauges are mounted in a neat column to the left of the flight instruments, with the various other dials scattered about. In common with many other British fighter designs, the stick articulates at about the midpoint. It is quite tall, because as the controls are purely mechanical (no hydraulic-boost) the stick loads are quite heavy at high indicated airspeeds. A long control stick gives the pilot more leverage.

For the right-seat pilot, the elevator trim wheel, throttle and flap lever are situated on a neat centre console that extends aft between the ejector seats. This also carries the HP fuel cock and two large buttons (one red, the other green), which operate the undercarriage. For the P1 all the controls detailed above (except HP fuel cock) are duplicated and situated on the left cockpit sidewall.

With the ejection seat's safety pins stowed, Tom presses the starter button, the engine rpm winds up towards 15%, and somewhere behind us igniters crackle and fuel turns to flame, flooding through the engine. The revs continue to rise, the JPT needle springs to life and we watch intently to ensure it doesn't exceed 710°C, and settles below 600. Outside, a banshee-like screech splits the air as the jet idles and Tom completes the post-start checks. With the numerous gauges indicating that the systems are functioning normally, Tom presses a button, the canopy smoothly slides shut and we set off. The nosewheel only castors, so directional control on the ground is by differential braking and rudder. It's quite a long taxi to the runway, and although we started with 2,000lbs showing on the gauge, by the time we are ready to line up I'm sure that the needle has dipped fractionally. All jet engines have an almost insatiable thirst at low level, and even taxiing out at idle rpm consumes about 6lbs/minute (the fuel gauge is in pounds). Before lining up we review the takeoff brief and ejection envelope. These Mk.4 seats are cleared for 0ft/90kt; they have a ground-level ejection capability, provided that the airspeed is above 90kt and the aircraft is in level or climbing flight. Therefore, below 90 we will stop on the runway, while an emergency above that speed will require immediate ejection. My straps are already tight, but I instinctively give them an extra tug

The takeoff run in a jet is a very different experience from flying, for example, a powerful taildragger. There is no thrashing prop, roaring motor or airframe vibrations – just a sensation of something spinning somewhere behind you, which is generating inexorable thrust. One final bump and we're airborne, a quick dab of the brakes to stop the still-spinning wheels, and I press the large red 'retract undercarriage' button while gently checking forwards to hold the aircraft down until we have 200kt. The wheels fold neatly away into the seamless metal skin with three delicate thuds, and we continue to accelerate. As the needle of the ASI reaches 200kt, I ease the stick back to hold that speed and the Strikemaster begins climbing like a rocket. I am momentarily confused when, despite blipping the button on the stick top back, the stick forces in pitch remained unchanged. Tom laughingly points out that the button on the stick top actually fires the rockets, and the large trim wheel is the only way to trim the aircraft in pitch. After a fantastic flight, its back to Duxford to see if I can land it. Established on downwind at 1,000ft and 150kt for a left-hand circuit to Runway 24, I ease the power back while maintaining altitude, then as the airspeed dips below 140kt, press the large green button to lower the undercarriage. As the wheels extend into the airflow I nudge the power up to compensate for the increased drag while concentrating on holding 140kt and 1,000ft. The jet trembles slightly as the wheels lock into place, the first stage of flap goes down, and the speed bleeds back to 125kt. As I am sitting in the right-hand seat I lose sight of the runway as I pass the numbers, but Tom tells me when to turn base. Established on final, with the airspeed sinking towards the target airspeed of 115kt, the approach feels slightly flat, but this is because it is vital to maintain at least 55%. Below 55% it will take several seconds for the engine to 'spool up', and until it does the aircraft will continue to sink. If you're more used to flying piston-powered propeller-driven aeroplanes, this is most certainly an important point to bear in mind! Under Tom's prompting I pull the power off as we cross the fence and round out. The first landing works reasonably well, and I smoothly increase the power for a touch-and-go. As we're still travelling at about 80kt we accelerate rapidly down the runway and back into the air. Dab the brakes, press the button, and we're quickly approaching 1,000ft as I'm swinging the Strikemaster onto the downwind leg. Under Tom's careful tutelage this second circuit is a tidier affair than the first, and I'm already feeling increasingly confident. After another reasonable landing, I open the throttle for a third and final circuit. This time it all clicks into place. Tom is not only a successful businessman and fine pilot but he is also an excellent instructor – and I notice with surprise that I'm at exactly 1,000ft and 150kt as we commence the downwind leg.

I still need his help in calling the base leg, as I simply can't see the runway, but the speeds and heights at the various parts of the circuit have become more precise as I'm setting the power much more quickly and accurately. The needle of the ASI is nailed to the 125kt mark on base, and it drops neatly back to *exactly* 115 on final. A squeeze of throttle to arrest the sink rate, pinch it back off on short final and then ease it back to the stop as we sail over the fence. Round out, wait and the mainwheels sink softly onto the tarmac. I ease off the back pressure on the stick, and with a gentle jolt the nosewheel is suddenly rumbling along the runway. What a day – but I want more and – almost a decade later, get the chance.

On a brisk and blustery day at North Weald I meet up with Tom to fly Strikemaster G-CFBK. This is an ex-Saudi Air Force Mk80A, although confusingly it is in Kuwaiti Air Force markings. Strapped in and started up, we follow the Jet Provost cameraship out to the runway. The JP accelerates away, and although we've given it a good head start, it is immediately apparent that we have a lot more thrust – about 40% to be precise. The Jet Provost is often described unkindly as having 'constant thrust-variable noise', but BAC designed the Strikemaster to be operated from relatively short, unprepared strips. Even at MAUW it can be airborne in fewer than 500m. It is considerably more powerful than its training cousin, but the underwing pylons mean it has a lot more drag. Consequently, although we accelerate faster, take off quicker and climb better than the JP, once straight and level the JP is clearly faster as it has much less drag. Tom slips smoothly into formation and our tight two-ship formation heads east at 220kt. There's a lot of cloud about, but we eventually find a large enough hole in which to do some formation loops. Steve and Tom are flying precisely, like the consummate professionals they are, and it shows. But we have an interesting problem. We need a hole that will enable us to loop in formation without pulling too much G (otherwise, Keith's camera will get very heavy!), and at the same time we need to stay below 10,000ft. Tom is concentrating hard, but I know he's enjoying himself immensely, and as we zoom up into another loop he suddenly says, "this is just such great fun" – and I can only agree with him. It really is tremendous sport! Unfortunately, the fuel state is constantly diminishing, and soon the gauge indicates a return to North Weald would be prudent, particularly as we're a fair way down wind – and it's pretty windy.

Back on the ground at North Weald we refuel and then taxi out for another flight. Our original plan was for me to fly a few circuits. However, it's still blustery and the tower advises that the wind is now "290 at 28, gusting 35". As North Weald has a

Runway 31 this shouldn't be a problem, but the airfield management has closed it for the day. Consequently, we must use 02, which has a near 90° crosswind that is gusting up to 35kt! Neither of us fancies me practising touch 'n' goes in these conditions (after all, I haven't flown a Strikey for ten years), so we quickly modify the plan. Tom will take us off and I'll fly us out to the practice area where we'll take turns in rehearsing Tom's display. we scorch across the sky to Osea Island which we'll use as the display line. There's still a lot of cloud, so Tom runs through his 'flat show', which consists of a flowing sequence of aileron and barrel rolls, with a graceful wing over at each end. I try to keep it smooth and flowing – but I'm not sure what the imaginary crowd would've made of my initial efforts. Tom is a fine and patient instructor, and after a few more goes I can sense that my display is getting a bit tidier – although I've still got a great deal of practicing to do before I can compete with him! His manoeuvres are so graceful that they seem effortless, and the 'g' comes on so smoothly and steadily. In fact, I don't think we ever pulled more than about 4.5g. However, unlike when flying something like an Extra (in which the 'g' can be intense and immediate, but is generally only transitory) in a jet you can easily pull a *sustained* +6g, which is much more wearing. The trick to avoid 'greying out' (as we weren't wearing G-suits) is to strain and grunt. It's not attractive, but it does work! Tom recommends 250kt for an aileron roll and 300 for a barrel, and to ensure that the nose is well up at the start. As the g's come on I sink down onto my ejection seat. A bit more throttle to keep the rpm at 95%, then I keep rolling and pulling up, and up into a barrel roll. Sea and sky swap places as the Strikemaster slices through the sky, and after a full 360 I level the wings to the horizon and ease the power back. "How's that?" I ask. "Better!" Tom replies, and I know he's grinning under his oxygen mask. "Not good – but better!"

By coincidence I'd been reading *Storm Front,* which details how Strikemasters played a pivotal role in the defence of Mirbat in Oman during 1972. As I curve the Strikey around in a graceful wingover and the island fills the windscreen it is easy to imagine rolling in on a target and firing a salvo of SURA rockets. However, I can't really imagine doing it below a 300ft cloud base!

I could stay airborne all day, but low-level aerobatics mean the fuel is flowing to the engine like water through a fire hose. As the fuel gauge dips below the 1,000lb mark it's clearly time to go back. Tom likes to be 'on the chocks' with 400lbs remaining, and I can see why. At low level, turbojets like the Viper really drink fuel, and even a slight delay (such as an aircraft with a burst tyre blocking the runway for a few minutes) can quickly turn a drama into a crisis! I fly us back to North Weald, chucking in a few more rolls on the way, and then enter the circuit for a 'run and break' with 700lbs left. To be honest, I'm a bit slow with the throttle and nearly cock this simple manoeuvre up – only some timely prompting from Tom stops me busting Stansted's airspace, as above North Weald its base is only 1,300ft. The windsock is thrashing around like a fish on a line as we turn final, but despite the powerful crosswind Tom makes a fine landing. I am impressed.

As we come to a stop outside the hangar Tom opens the canopy, closes the high-pressure cock, and the Viper dies away with an ever-decreasing whine. Oil and hydraulic pressures fall, lights flicker and fade, and gyros slowly spin down as the *Strikey* morphs from a fire-breathing creature of the air into a disparate collection of metal, plastic and rubber.

Chapter 3
Banner Tow

As I drop down to 50ft I'm acutely aware that the difference between my mainwheels hitting the banner pick-up loop and the grappling hook missing the loop is about five feet. The supporting poles, which had initially been quite difficult to spot in the low sun suddenly loom in the windscreen. Simultaneously, I push the throttle open and pull the stick back. The engine roars and the Chipmunk rockets skywards – have I missed? A long second, then I feel a firm tug through the seatback. Got it!

This particular caper had started several weeks earlier, when restrictions on flying were first lifted. I'd been chatting at a socially distanced two metres with the owner of Chipmunk Mk.23 `Bumblemunk' Richard Ellingworth, when he'd suddenly said "do you think you could tow a banner with *Bumblemunk*?" "From an operational perspective, I don't see why not" I'd replied "but we'd have to look into the legalities. Why do you ask?" "Well" he explained, "everybody at my company worked right through lockdown, supplying local businesses. Most of them were quite worried about Covid-19, but everyone always turned up – and I think it really helped their morale to know that the NHS had their backs. I'd like to do something to show support for the health service" he continued "tell you what, can you find out if it can be done? And if it can, I'll buy a banner-towing kit. Will you tow it?" "Of course," I replied. "Several of my friends or their partners work for the NHS, so deal me in!" After a flurry of emails with the very-helpful CAA GA unit it transpired that indeed it could be done, so the banner was ordered and the game afoot!

I really like flying the Chipmunk Mk.23. It has the perfect blend of controllability and stability, a powerful, responsive engine, beautifully harmonized controls, good speed stability and a fine field of view. It'd be nice if it had a bit more endurance, as the two 41-litre tanks aren't really enough for a Lycoming O-360, and this became increasingly obvious when we started considering various routes. Initially we designed a track with multiple targets, but it soon became apparent that (in a damning indictment of the way successive governments have run down the NHS) the Mk.23 simply didn't have the range to safely tow the banner past more than two hospitals on the same flight. The nearest hospital to Saltby is Grantham's, and as the locals have been battling to keep its A&E department open and there's a regular protest outside the gates most Thursdays it seemed entirely apposite to 'wave the flag' there.

Of course, the 'Devil's in the detail' and I planned carefully. It's pointless flying over the town, as half of the people won't be able to read it. The trick is to fly several orbits around the periphery to ensure maximum readability, while also ensuring I could 'glide clear' in the event of an engine failure. I then realized that to ensure the good people outside the hospital could read it I'd need to fly quite close to Barkston Heath's ATZ, which is of course 24/7. But is Barkston's ATZ 2NM, or 2.5? Well, the runway doesn't look that long, but I'm glad I checked, because the delineating factor is, as all Pilot's readers undoubtedly know, whether or not the longest runway is more than 1,850m – and Barkston's is 1,868! The next potential pitfall was the beautiful 12th century church of St Wulfram's. To stay legal, I'd have to remain 1000ft vertically and 600m laterally from the nearest structure, and at 283ft St Wulfram's is the third tallest parish church spire in England. The temptation was to simply add on several hundred feet for the sake of my licence, but then no one would be able to read the banner. The answer? Precision flying, and not just vertically and laterally, but my speed control would also require exactitude. I soon learnt that at 60kt the oil temperature began to creep up, while at 70kt the banner could start to tear.

As it transpired, all went well. Having successfully snatched the banner off the ground I set off for Grantham on a gorgeous June evening at 65kt, and flew several orbits of the town. It's real finger-tip flying and requires a high level of concentration, but it's good fun – and also very rewarding when (for example) you spot a group of people in a park, and they're all pointing and waving. It may seem corny, but as I flew slowly across the evening sky I hoped that somewhere down there a student nurse, veteran doctor or any of the myriad health workers that had literally put their lives on the line during the pandemic looked up, saw the 'WE♥NHS' and got a kick out of it. I hoped so, but didn't know. Having dropped the banner and landed I could see that Richard was all smiles, and as the prop slowed to a stop I slid the canopy back and turned my phone on, and it beeped, buzzed and pinged with multiple message alerts. Such is the power of social media that news of the flight (including photos) was all over Facebook, even before I'd landed! Practically every single one of the notes was positive, with the only complaints being that they hadn't seen it, and when would it happen again? We've subsequently towed a bigger 72♥NHS banner over several other towns and hospitals. It's taking both time and fuel, but if it put a smile on the face of the Great British Public (well, those who live in Northamptonshire, Leicestershire, Lincolnshire and Rutland), then it was well worth it.

Chapter 4
North American TP-51C Mustang

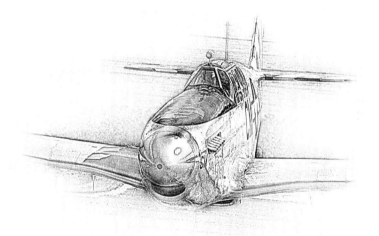

Clear prop! The starter whines and the giant four-blade prop slowly begins to revolve. A couple of cylinders catch, stumble and fire again. The mighty Merlin roars into life and the prop dissolves into a shining, shimmering blur as smoke streams down the fuselage. The RPM and my BPM rise together. As you might expect when flying a machine like the Mustang, fuel and adrenaline flow are all closely related – and increase exponentially whenever the throttle is opened. Coolant and cockpit temperatures can also be an issue! Having greatly enjoyed flying the Collings Foundation's B-17 Fortress, B-24 Liberator and B-25 Mitchell, I was thrilled to be offered the chance to fly one of its famous fighters, the P-51. Not just any Mustang but the ultra-rare TP-51C *Betty Jane*.

I was expecting to fly with my old mate Jim Harley, the Collings Wings of Freedom Tour's Chief Pilot, but as things turn out, Jim is needed to fly the B-24, so I fly with Mark Murphy. Knowledgeable and likeable, Mark has over 500 hours in P-51s - his family owns one - and indicates that he's happy for me to try a takeoff and landing from the back seat. I just don't have enough T-6 time to fly from the front.

Betty Jane has been safely ensconced in a hangar overnight and as she emerges into the warm morning sun, the principal difference between a P-51C and the later D-model is obvious. Whereas the latter has a large bubble canopy, the former is fitted with a multi-pane arrangement that wouldn't look out of place on a contemporary Luftwaffe aircraft.

The 'razorback' Mustang also has some more subtle differences. For example, the leading edge of the fin, where it joins the fuselage, is very different to the 'D, which just has a small dorsal fillet. The heart of the Mustang is one of the finest – and most famous – piston engines ever made; the Rolls-Royce Merlin V-12. Built under licence by Packard, this particular version is a V-1650-7, and produces up to 1,595hp (1,189kW) at 3,000rpm. It is fed from four wing tanks, two in each wing, with a combined capacity of 681 litres.

It's a bit of climb up to the cockpit, using several well-located handholds and 'kick-in' steps. Although I wasn't going to fly it from the front cockpit, I couldn't resist having a quick sit in it. The layout of the controls and instruments isn't brilliant, but by the standards of the time, not bad either. The stick and throttle both fall nicely to hand, while the rudder pedals adjust over a good range. The prop and mixture controls are mounted adjacent to the throttle, with the trim wheels, flap and undercarriage levers underneath.

Securely strapped into the rear seat and my parachute, I begin to study my surroundings more closely and immediately realise that although the canopy is still open, I can already see (or rather *not* see) that the field of view from the back seat is certainly compromised.

Somewhat surprisingly, the instrument panel is quite badly laid out. Indeed, the location of the primary flying instruments is far from being the standard 'six-pack', as the Directional Gyro (DG) is where the airspeed indicator (ASI) should be, the ASI sits in the normal DG spot, and the compass is where you'd expect to find the turn and slip indicator. The altimeter is of the modern single pointer/counter drum type, and, of course, all the avionics are digital and include dual GPS. There are also quite a few warning and status lights scattered around the panel, with the critical ones (coolant temperature, oil pressure and temperature and fuel pressure) mounted in a neat column outboard of the manifold pressure gauge and tachometer. A row of orange lights show which fuel tank is selected. Apart from the somewhat unusual arrangement of the flight instruments and zero view forwards, I soon begin to feel quite comfortable in the cockpit. As with some of the other North American types that I've flown – such as the T-6 and T-28 Trojan, although at first glance it looks a bit cluttered, closer inspection reveals that it is reasonably well-designed, with the various systems and sub-systems all laid out logically.

Before start-up, the canopy is closed, but unlike the elegant one-piece 'bubble' of the TF-51D, the TP-51C's is a much more cumbersome affair. An interlocking 'clamshell' design, it consists of four separate parts, excluding the windscreen.

Almost immediately the cockpit temperature begins to rise, and I hurriedly slide open the side window.

With the mighty Merlin grumbling powerfully to itself we complete the post-start checks and begin to taxi out behind the B-24. As soon as we begin to move I realise the field of view is very poor, and made even worse because the clamshell canopy must be closed prior to engine start-up, so you can't even stick your head out of the side to get a better view.

When it is on the ground in the 'three-point' attitude, I'd say the view forwards is practically non-existent and because of the long cowling I'm sure it isn't great from the front seat, so 'S-turning' is essential.

The tailwheel steers through the rudder pedals up to 6-degrees either side if the stick is held back past the neutral position. Pushing the stick forwards to the panel unlocks the tailwheel and allows it to castor, differential braking can then be used for tighter turns.

Mark encourages me to taxi and although initially I'm rather nervous as I really can't see much, in a blinding flash of clarity, I suddenly have a great idea. Mark has a much better view than me, and he's not going to let me do anything that might even remotely jeopardise this priceless machine.

All I have to do is take my time, do my best and let him fix any mistakes.

Emboldened, I taxi out to the run-up area slowly but confidently. The taxiway lights are typically around 30m apart, so a good tip is to make an S-turn just after you pass one. That way you know it's behind you, so if you do swing slightly wide you don't hit it.

Having been lucky enough to fly a Spitfire Tr.9 a couple of times, I am well aware of just how quickly the Merlin's coolant (a mixture of water and ethylene glycol) can get dangerously hot, and as the outside air temperature is distinctly warm I study the coolant temperature gauge with particular interest. However, the Mustang's system is much better designed and the coolant stays – well, cool. That said, the cockpit was rapidly heating up.

At the run-up point, Mark talks me through the pre-take-off checks, and emphasised the importance of correct use of rudder trim. The flaps are usually left 'Up', although if runway length is an issue, up to 20-degrees can be used. With the oil temperature above 40°C and the coolant nearer 60°C I increase power to 2,300rpm, check the mags and cycle the prop.

Having taxied out onto the runway I line-up just to the right of the centreline (so I've got at least a vague reference), roll forward a few metres to ensure the tailwheel is straight, and then smoothly - but a little too slowly - open the throttle up to 40ins of manifold pressure.

Although I knew the throttle friction ring would be wound down pretty tight, the throttle really is quite stiff. I don't want to force it and initially we just 'gather speed' rather than accelerate. On the plus side, the Mustang doesn't swing. As the needle of the ASI sweeps past 50kt I hold the stick in the neutral position and the tailwheel gently rises. Increase power to 50ins MP, check the tachometer needle is hovering above the '30' mark and now we're really accelerating. The noise is phenomenal, and the Mustang soon slides into the sky in a slightly tail-low attitude. Undercarriage lever to 'Up' and as soon as the wheels are in the wells Mark tells me to reduce power to 40ins and 2,500rpm while he sets the cooling system to 'Auto'. The optimum coolant temperature is around 100°C, and the coolant gauge is a vital part of a Mustang driver's instrument scan. Now that we're airborne my field of view has improved considerably. The bubble canopy of the P-51D makes you feel as if you're almost sitting *on* the fuselage –but with the 'C you're definitely aware that you're sitting *in* it. We soon level off and Mark tells me to set cruise power of 35in/ 2,350rpm. We soon catch up with the B-24 and Mark takes control and moves into formation. As we close in on the big bomber, I fully appreciate just what a fat target a B-24 must've been in a Focke-Wulf Fw 190 or Messerschmitt Bf 109 gunsight. If you could get in close without being shot down you couldn't miss. We then wave goodbye to the bomber's occupants and climb up over Florida's giant Lake Okeechobee so I can try some aerobatics. With the power back up to 40ins and 2,500rpm we climb at 170kt and 3,000ft/min so it doesn't take long to reach 8,000ft. Mark encourages me to acquaint myself with the machine's general handling characteristics, so while still scorching skywards I try a few steep turns. The primary controls are powerful and although any out-of-trim condition produces forces that are quite high, they are easily trimmed out. Harmony of control is good with the ailerons being the lightest and the rudder the heaviest. As Mark warned, the slip ball needed to be monitored constantly, and rudder applied judiciously. As long as you trim regularly and always keep the speed above at least 150kt - to provide a sensible cushion - aerobatting a Mustang is tremendous fun.

Unlike modern competition aerobatic aircraft, its size and weight mean that things happen relatively slowly, except for acceleration. Once the nose is well below the horizon it really accelerates, and at altitude probably soon runs into compressibility. Under Mark's patient tutelage, I try a couple of loops and rolls, including aileron and barrel, before finishing off with a pretty good four-point roll, and a not-so-good eight-point version.

It's nearly time to land at Okeechobee airport, but first Mark can't resist taking control and descending for a high-speed low-level run over the lake. Racing at 250kts across the water gives me a good idea of what a strafing run must feel like, but using high power at low level really gobbles the gas. Turning downwind at Okeechobee, I ease the throttle back to 24ins with the prop at 2,500rpm, set the flaps to 20 degrees and concentrate on maintaining 140kt. The undercarriage then goes down, along with another ten degrees of flap and some nose-up trim; speed 130.

If I can fly a neat, curving base leg I should be able to keep the runway more or less in sight until short final, so as soon as we're abeam the numbers I start turning. The last 10 degrees of flap goes down, along with more nose-up trim and some right rudder trim (in case of a go-around); speed 120. On very short final I roll the wings level with the speed bleeding back towards 105, and as we flash over the fence I glance at the ASI and see exactly 100kts. As the nose is still pitched well down I can see the runway over Mark's shoulder, but as soon as I raise the nose and start easing the throttle back my view forward shrinks to zero. I firmly focus my peripheral vision on the runway's edge and continue easing the stick and throttle back while knowing Mark is poised to take control if things even look like going awry.

The Merlin pops and crackles as we sink, then a combination of good luck, excellent coaching and 3,000 hours of tailwheel time sees the mainwheels chirp gently onto the concrete, followed by the tailwheel. All I can see is the side of the runway, but it's enough to tell me we're running straight so I simply hold the stick back and let the Mustang keep rolling along with just a few quick dabs of rudder. The runway is free, but the brakes are expensive so I wait until the '1,000ft' marker flicks past the canopy, then slip my toes further up the pedals and just think about braking. I take the turn-off at walking speed while Mark retracts the flaps and opens the radiator door fully. "Great job," he says, adding: "If we fly together again I'll put you in the front." I'm well chuffed.

As we approach the parking ramp there's the usual small cluster of elderly, dignified men in well-worn A2 jackets, standing by the B-17 and B-24. As we pull up alongside I notice one veteran clearly struggling to control his emotions. I've seen this before when taxying historic aircraft and I always think the same thoughts – I know what he's looking at, but what does he *see*? A piece of history, or a piece of his story?

Chapter 5
Where The Sea Meets The Sky

I've always been fascinated by the sea, almost as much as the sky, and even spending several months sailing around the Bering Sea on a trawler in the mid-80s didn't put me off. I think that the sea – even more than the sky – exercises an almost primeval fascination on many of us, possibly because the earliest forms of life came from the ocean, or maybe even because we live on an island. And there's a more prosaic view for aviators;- air and water are both fluids, and if you can visualise how water behaves when it hits a rock in a fast-flowing stream it will definitely help you understand curl-over from a stand of trees, mountain wave and even mechanical turbulence off a poorly-sited hangar.

Today, my 14-year-old son George is First Mate, and we're planning to fly the SF-25 to and along the Lincolnshire coast. As we depart the Saltby circuit we continue the climb to take advantage of the following wind. The SF-25 has many fine facets, but speed isn't one of them and – just like the old sailors – we must use the wind to our advantage whenever possible. Another of George's tasks is Navigation Officer, and I emphasise how important it is that he doesn't let us drift too close to the RAF airfields of Barkston Heath, Cranwell and Coningsby on our way to the coast. (No GPS for us, today we're doing things 'old school', with chart, compass, and chronometer.) In fact, the navigation is easy – there's a huge windfarm due south of Coningsby, and we keep that well off our port wing until we see the 'Boston Stump' (AKA St Botolph's). At 83m high it is one of the three tallest medieval towers in England, and has long been a landmark for airmen and sailors alike, as on a clear day it can be seen from East Anglia, on the other side of The Wash. Now we can see the confluence where the rivers Haven and Welland merge to meet the sea, so with absolute certainty of our position (as the Holbeach Danger Area is quite close) we turn onto a northerly heading and sail our motorised sailplane along the coast. The wind is slowly drifting us out to sea but as the SF-25 has a 'best glide' of about 24:1 I'm not too concerned, until the legendary 'auto-rough' setting that affects all single-engine aircraft flying over the sea manifests itself. Is that a new noise? Temperatures and pressures are all good, but I still take the aircraft's 'pulse' by barely nipping the top of the control column between thumb and forefinger and feeling for any unusual vibration. All is well, but nevertheless I edge back towards the coast. The sea is calm and peaceful today, yet I know that it is capable of tremendous, almost malevolent, violence. I will never forget being out in the Bering in a really big storm. There was a nor'westerly blowing at Force 10, the wind was howling and screaming in the rigging and waves higher than the wheelhouse were rolling past. It was one of those nights when – as Gordon Lightfoot wrote in 'The Wreck of the Edmund Fitzgerald – that "the waves turn the minutes to hours". At one point even the skipper looked worried, so you can imagine how I felt. But back to today. No sea-story worth its salt is complete without a shipwreck and this one is no exception – in fact there are at least two. South of Gibraltar Point George spots two semi-submerged hulks and the outline of a third in the shoals, on the very edge of the Boston Deeps. They aren't the rotting relics of some terrible tragedy or naval battle though, but the decaying evidence of the old Wainfleet bombing range. Mind you, I'm sure George desperately wants to believe that they *are* shipwrecks, although the fact they have been repeatedly attacked by RAF and USAF fighter-bombers is nearly as interesting to him!

Beyond the wrecks, sea and sky merge into an endless blue nothingness. It's hard to see where the sky starts and the sea stops, but below our broad wings the colour of the sea's surface is much more subtle, with various shades of cobalt, indigo, cerulean and sapphire. As a colour palette its imperfection is – well – perfect. The coast is very low-lying here, and with the tide on the ebb and the relatively low sun sparkling off the rippling waves it's a positively pastoral picture. Athwart Gibraltar Point we simultaneously climb and head back out to sea to avoid the bird sanctuary. The tide is ebbing fast now, the shoals of Wainfleet Sands are already beginning to show, and the shape of the coastline is changing by the minute. George is intrigued by the massive wind farm that sprouts from the sea abeam Skegness, but my gaze is drawn to the azure emptiness to the north-east. The SF has a very large fuel tank, and somewhere over the blue horizon lay the coastlines of Germany, Norway, Sweden, and The Netherlands. Perhaps one day we'll set a course out across the North Sea on a real adventure, but not today. I swing the nose back towards shore and start a gradual descent. The voyage home will be straight into wind, and while we won't have to tack to make headway our progress will be greatly enhanced if I can reduce the headwind component. Eventually our 'home port' of Saltby comes into view, and within minutes we're outside our hangar. I tell George to turn off the single magneto;- "Finished with engines, Number One!" He flicks the switch, and the prop slows to a stop. "Finished with engines, aye aye dad."

Chapter 6
De Havilland DH.90 Dragonfly

Walking across the wet grass to the Dragonfly gleaming in the wan light of an overcast autumn morning I'm struck by just how incredibly beautiful an aircraft it is, and also how appositely it is named. While we'd been waiting for the rain to stop Henry Labouchere had claimed that "..it's a Renoir, a Matisse of an aeroplane", and with the sun just starting to illuminate it I fully understand what he means. An Art

Deco masterpiece with wings, it's absolutely gorgeous.

As we begin the pre-flight I realise that there isn't a better person to introduce me to the Dragonfly than Henry. Not only is he one of the most experienced exponents of DH biplanes (both as a pilot and engineer) in the world, he also restored Delta Uniform and literally knows it inside out. Access to the engines is good, as the nacelles hinge open on both sides to reveal a brace of de Havilland Gipsy Major 10 Mk.1-IIIs. These air-cooled inverted in-fours produce 145hp each at 2,450rpm and turn wooden two-blade fixed-pitch Hoffman props.

As they don't feather losing an engine could certainly be construed as inconvenient, although as we're light Henry says it will maintain height and might even climb. However, at MAUW on a hot day "the best you can hope for is an engine assisted descent, preferably into a satisfactory field". On the plus side, operating 'off piste' wouldn't be too onerous, because as it was conceived when even large international airports were unpaved the main wheels and tailwheel are quite large and the undercarriage track wide. Ailerons are on the top wing only, while the two-piece split flaps are located between the engine nacelles. They don't look as if they'd be especially effective at generating additional lift, and Henry confirms that they are primarily drag producers. The fin looks slightly on the small side, although the mass-balanced rudder is quite large. The curvaceous tailplane carries a broad-chord elevator and I note the absence of trim tabs with interest. The electrical system are powered by an air-driven generator set into the port upper wing's leading edge.

With the walk-round complete we climb up into the cockpit via a large door on the port side. It's a big step up, so there's a sort of metal stirrup next to it, which is blown up into trail by the air loads when in flight. An interesting feature is the large vertical bar just inside the door. It's a rather curious item, and Henry said that John Cunningham told him that it is a post-design fix for a minor torsional problem. While probably the least elegant aspect of the whole aeroplane it clearly fixed the problem and is also "jolly handy" when climbing in.

The interior is surprisingly spacious, and features a bench at the back, a single seat in the middle and two pilot's chairs. It is also well-lit as there are no less than nine separate transparencies for the cockpit, and a further two windows on either side of the cabin. The baggage bay is behind the bench seat and is accessed via a huge door on the starboard side just aft of the wings. Having settled onto the left seat with the help of some strategically placed cushions (the seat is "somewhat adjustable", but cushions are more efficacious) I acquaint myself with the layout of the instruments and controls. The panel is typically British and consists of myriad black dials set into a black panel. As for controls, the pilot has an inverted 'W' type yoke suspended from a crossbeam carried by a large column that rises from the floor, while the throttles and mixtures are mounted on the left cockpit sidewall with the tailwheel lock selector underneath. This is a Henry-modification (he's a firm believer in tailwheel locks) and as the type has a predilection to ground-loop it seems prudent.

An interesting aspect of operating old aeroplanes is that sometimes the controls move rather a long way – and the Dragonfly is no exception. The control yoke – and also the throttles –travel over quite a range. Big, silver button-topped levers on either side of the control column operate the elevator trim and flaps; there are three flap positions - Up, Take Off and Land. Henry emphasised that although he rarely uses any flap for takeoff, full flap is always used for landing, and that there is a significant change in pitch trim when the flaps are lowered or raised. Pitch trim is provided by a spring-bias system, but trimming in yaw is almost never done, as it's very difficult to reach the rudder trimmer (a small handle by the co-pilots left ankle). This is also a spring-bias arrangement. Henry likened its use - if you can reach it, I couldn't - to "like winding up a clockwork train".

In between the seats is a surprisingly complicated looking fuel selector panel, which has two levers (each with four positions!) for the two main 136-litre tanks plus an on/off selector for the 114-litre auxiliary tank at the back of the cabin. It is so complicated that a set of very comprehensive instructions regarding its operation are printed on a large placard on the cockpit wall. With all three tanks full the range is an impressive 885 miles, but the rear tank can only be utilised if the load in the cabin is substantially reduced. On wing tanks alone the still-air range is 625 miles.

Both engines start with a discrete cough and a faint puff of smoke as the prop blades fan into a blur. The panel comes to life as the oil pressures rise, the artificial horizon wobbles on its bearings and the aircraft begins the miraculous transformation from a disparate collection of wood, fabric, rubber and metal into a living, breathing flying machine, 76-years young.

Fuel and oil are coursing through its veins, a crackle in my headset indicates that the intercom is working and I can feel the propwash drumming insistently against the elevator through the yoke. It's eager to fly, so touch the throttles forward and set off towards the downwind side of the aerodrome. The field of view over the nose is good and the undercarriage feels quite well damped as we taxi slowly across the wet grass with the engines chuffing contently to themselves. When unlocked the tailwheel only castors, so steering is by deft, delicate touches of differential brake and throttle.

At the run-up point we run through the pre-take off checks, test the mags and discuss the various speeds and rpms. Having flown a few old aeroplanes I'm aware that many of them have a 'magic number' (essentially, the same speed is used for several different phases of flight) and the Dragonfly is no exception – 65kt is the speed for Vy, Vyse and Vref.

As I swing carefully into wind and reach down to lock the tailwheel I'm slightly uneasy about flying something quite so extraordinary. It is also the only airworthy DH.90 in the Northern Hemisphere, and although Henry is in the other seat he has neither brakes nor throttles. As if sensing my trepidation he reminds me that "it's not

52

difficult, just different" – and I know he's right. Roll forward a couple of metres to ensure that the tailwheel has locked into trail, advance the throttles smoothly and the muted muttering of the motors swells to a roar as the Dragonfly begins to gather speed. Acceleration is quite good with just a slight tendency to swing. Ease the yoke forward a long way to pick the tailwheel up as the airspeed comes alive, then back to neutral. Catch the incipient swing with a boot full of rudder, the wings take the weight and suddenly we're flying, skimming low across the grass as we wait for the airspeed to reach 65 before easing up into the climb. Climbing away at 65kt the VSI is showing well over 750fpm, so at 500ft I reduce power, then draw the port throttle slightly further back (the port engine revs about 50rpm faster than the starboard) to 'synch the props' while simultaneously lowering the nose and letting the airspeed build. Thus far the handling had been somewhat underwhelming, with the ailerons in particular feeling rather spongy. However as the speed increases a subtle but significant transformation in its character occurs and it becomes very nice indeed. I mention this to Henry who agrees, saying that "it doesn't like to go slow".

While sitting stationary and lifeless on the ground the Dragonfly had been merely a machine, albeit an aesthetically attractive one. But now it's alive and where it should be; - up in the sky. As the speed builds I'm already starting to sense some of its personality and character. It's a real 'Gentleman's Aerial Carriage' and the absolute epitome of aeronautical elegance. It positively oozes class. With a couple of thousand feet beneath our elegantly-tapered wings I swing the Dragonfly into a great sweeping circle above the Cotswolds. My initial impression of a fair field of view is reinforced in flight, while the controls feel nicely balanced, with little 'stiction' in the control circuits and low breakout forces. It's also more nimble than I'd expected, with the handling (especially in roll) much tauter. As with so many aeroplanes of this era, it likes plenty of rudder, but it definitely doesn't feel like a 1930s design, which can often have distinctly dissonant handling. The controls have plenty of authority, and even quite steep turns are handled with aplomb, although its does need a big handful of power and plenty of back pressure to stop from sinking once the bank angle goes much past 30°. An assessment of its stick-free stability is quite tricky, as the decidedly forward CG (we have no passengers and the aft-mounted auxiliary tank only contains about 20 litres) means that the pitch trim lever is on the backstop, while the air is slightly bumpy.

With about 2,050rpm set I think that the 90kt cruise is pretty fair, but Henry gruffly announces that he can make it do another eight knots at the same rpm – and he does. Suitably chastised, I vow to pay more attention to T&S indicator. It's also interesting to note how smooth the Dragonfly is, although of course wooden airframes do absorb vibration better than metal. The next item on the flight test card is single-engine performance, so I gently close the port throttle, bank slightly into the 'good' engine and concentrate on maintaining exactly 65kt. As predicted, the Dragonfly responds with a shallow climb, although we really are quite light. One engine at MAUW on a hot day must be a real 'seat-chomping' experience.

Exploring slow flight is interesting. Now, you'd think that with all those wires, struts, trousers and wheels out there in the breeze there'd be plenty of drag, but this aircraft doesn't fly quite as you'd think – it's slipperier than it looks, and slowing down takes a while. With flaps up, the power at idle and a steady deceleration of one knot per second there is very little buffet until the wings just can't hold the weight at around 47kt. Dropping the flaps reinforces the points Henry emphasised on the ground;- there's a big change in pitch trim and the airspeed collapses. It rather reminds me of the Miles Magister. As expected, the flaps are primarily drag generators not lift producers, and the stall speed only reduces by about three knots. The Vfe is 74kt, but in deference to its age Henry recommends 65.

Cruising back towards Rendcomb at 3,000ft with the power set to 2,050rpm gives a TAS of 112kt for a fuel flow of about 55lit/hr. I'm really starting to feel more comfortable with the Dragonfly, and a glance at the T&S confirms the slip needle centred. All through the day Henry has been hugely enthusiastic about the Dragonfly and I can see why. What an aircraft! It's a real aristocrat of the air – an 'airistocraft' if you will – and if it could talk its accent would be distinctly 'Received Pronunciation'! With Rendcomb looming large in the windscreen it was time to start thinking about the landing. I've observed before that vintage machines are at their most idiosyncratic in the circuit, and the Dragonfly is no exception. With power and trim set for 65, when you lower the flaps (Henry recommends putting them all down in one go) it produces a significant change in pitch trim and a marked reduction in airspeed. Your control inputs are not entirely unlike being on a cross-trainer, because firstly your right hand pulls the flap lever back and your left pushes the yoke forward, then your left hand pulls the yoke back as your right pushes the trim forward. Then you swap hands on the yoke, and return your left to the throttles.

As Henry reiterated several times – it's not difficult, just different. Once it's back in trim and all the levers are where they should be it's simply a matter of using power and pitch as appropriate. Speed stability is good, and I take care to nail the speed to 65. Lose an engine below Vyse and not only will the bottom fall out of your world, but the world may fall out of your bottom! Start bleeding speed back to 60 on very short final and then chop the throttles over the hedge while drawing the yoke back.. and back.. and back. The controls certainly do have a long throw but (due mostly to Henry's coaching) we run out of speed, height and elevator at about the same time and the Dragonfly subsides gracefully onto the ground. I ask Henry if I can fly another circuit without any 'prompting from the wings' and he smilingly agrees. This time I'm ready for the swing as the tail comes up and the Dragonfly runs straight and true. Unfortunately I still make a bit of a pig's ear when flapping and trimming (it's not difficult, but it is *definitely* different) but everything is as it should as we swing onto base. We're correctly configured, the speed and angle are both right and – crucially – Henry says nothing. A final turn and the Dragonfly starts sliding down the imaginary slope that leads to the waiting aerodrome. I pinch some power off, then squeeze it back on again almost instantly. Henry says nothing. Over the hedge! Throttles and yoke back together. Wait ...wait...hold it....a bit of a bump, and we're down. The landing is slightly firmer than my first effort (I imagine that the Dragonfly probably feels it was a rather vulgar arrival, and its used to making an elegant entrance) but it's acceptable. I suspect that on flat ground and nil wind you can comfortably shave at least 5kt off 'over the hedge', but as the field has an upslope we need a little extra energy in the flare.

The engines stop as softly as a butler's apology, and I can almost picture Noel Coward lounging insouciantly on the bench seat. When asked if he'd enjoyed the flight he'd glance deprecatingly at Henry and I then reply "well, aeronautically it was a great success. Socially it left much to be desired!" As we slide the hangar doors closed I take one last lingering look at the de Havilland DH.90 Dragonfly. The 'limousine airliner'. The most beautiful biplane in the world.

Chapter 7
Scouts and Students

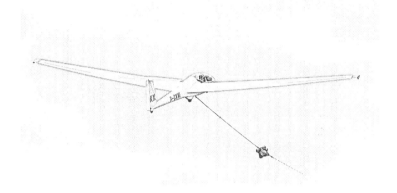

It's a beautiful summer's afternoon and my little Jodel's engine is humming happily as we hop over to Saltby, where I'm helping at a local Scout troop's flying evening. I've barely climbed out of the diminutive cockpit before a young girl wanders over to introduce herself, her eyes bright with enthusiasm. "We're here for the scout flying evening" she announces peremptorily "and I'm here early cos I want to go first." Eleven-year old Lily is as bright as a button, as sharp as a tack and the charming, confident side of precocious. She eyes *Buzz* with keen interest, and when I ask if she'd like to sample the cockpit she doesn't need asking twice. Having explained the controls and instruments I lift the tail up into the flying attitude and she grins delightedly. Having helped her out I make my excuses and go to check in with the duty instructor. Half an hour later and the troop of Melton Mowbray scouts are assembled and briefed at the launch point. I'm about to ask, "who's first" then realise it's completely unnecessary. Lily is already wearing her parachute and standing next to the K-21 with a very possessive air. There is no doubt who's first. Lily squeals with delight during the winch launch, and having wafted up to 2,000 feet in an evening thermal I encourage her to take control and she loves it, particularly when I hold my hands above my head to prove that only she is controlling the sailplane. She wants aerobatics but all I'm prepared to do is a steep spiral, and as we've already been airborne longer than we should have, put the K-21 in a tight corkscrew. For the first time that flight the rear cockpit goes quiet, so I ease off on the 'g' and level out. "Everything okay Lily?" I ask with a hint of trepidation. There's a pause then "I'm grinning so hard my jaw hurts" she giggles. "That was amazing!" As we turn final I realise that as we're landing on 07 and its already well into the evening our shadow is racing us to the runway. I point it out to

Lily, who is enchanted. Several hours later and *Buzz* and I are wending our weary way home through the pellucid sky with a certain sense of smug satisfaction. The flying evening has been a huge success. All the children (and some of the parents) flew at least once and there were several soaring flights. The children were fun, the parents and troop leaders appreciative and – most importantly - everyone had enjoyed themselves immensely, and safely. Lily's comment about her jaw hurting still has me chuckling as the patchwork fields basking in the late evening sun slip slowly under *Buzz's* broad wings. The air is like warm velvet and the light glorious –what a great evening.

A few months later and I'm back at the club to help fly another group. The briefing room is as packed as I've ever seen it, while the disproportionate amount of young faces means it must be Freshers Week at Loughborough University, and the Loughborough Student's Union Gliding Club is out in force. Club stalwarts Ben, Lucy and Emma have clearly done an excellent sell and there's been a gratifyingly large uptake of students eager to sample soaring flight. New CFI Lyn is keen to put as many aircraft on the launch point as possible, so to increase the number of two-seaters available I'm manning the privately-owned K-7, which owner Les kindly allows me to fly. This gives us four two-seat sailplanes and two motor gliders, and as the fleet is arrayed on the runway it's good to see such a full flight line so early on an autumn morning. Most of the students have eager, excited expressions (mixed with a little trepidation) so I shrug on a parachute and get flying. The launch point is bustling but well organised by the experienced students, and the launch rate slick. By mid-afternoon I've flown more than a few winch launches and aerotows, and although not tired could do with a break. However, the poor old tuggy has been busy too, and as my old granny often used to say that 'a change is as good as a rest' I hand the K-7 over to Les, jump in the EuroFox and fly a few tows, until everyone who wanted to fly has flown. It's been a long, tiring but fun day (even the weather cooperated) and all the freshers have experienced a winch launch, an aerotow, and a flight in a motor glider. I've lost count of how many I've done, but the high aerotows have granted the students a splendid vista across Lincolnshire, Leicestershire and Nottinghamshire, while the winch launches got their full attention. Indeed, with an acceleration of around two seconds from nought to sixty, and climb rates over 2,000fpm it still excites me! The weather next day is significantly less benign. There's a considerable crosswind on the main runway, and heavy showers forecast. The K-7 isn't mine, is tricky in a crosswind and I don't want to get it wet, so with regret tell the students it's not a K-7 day. "No problem Dave" says Manager Roy, "we need a driver for the T-61." This proves to be the catalyst for another fun day, while as the T-61 is self-supporting I can take a bit more time with each student. My first customer is Elaina and just like all the students she is smart, perceptive and engaging. With its fabric covering, big monowheel and spindly outriggers the T-61 looks (and is) quite an elderly design, and if I'm honest 'Foxtrot Romeo' does look a little tatty, but if Elena has any reservations she hides them well. We're soon rolling down the runway and one of the great advantages of the motor glider manifests itself. There's a big blue hole just downwind of the Belvoir ridge, and while I wouldn't fancy it in the K-7, the assurance and assistance of the engine allows me to exploit the weak wave that's forming the hole and climb above the clouds. It's quite gloomy low down but it's a different world up high, very pretty and extremely smooth. Elaina seems to enjoy the experience and quickly picks up controlling the aircraft in pitch and roll. Each student is limited to thirty minutes in the motor glider so we head back to Saltby for my next customer. Randa is waiting, and while strapping in excitedly reveals she's never flown, not even in an airliner. Whenever someone says they've never left the ground I always want to make their first-ever flight unforgettable, and we're quickly motoring confidently back towards the wave gap. The weak but steady lift is still there and we're soon soaring above a flawless white cloudscape illuminated by the golden glowing orb of the autumn sun, which is set like a yellow topaz in a brilliant sapphire sky. It looks amazing, and as we sail serenely along the face of the cloud with the engine barely ticking over I suddenly spot one of the best 'glories' I've ever seen and hurriedly point it out to Randa, who is enchanted by the shadow of the T-61 seemingly surrounded by a seamless circular rainbow. It really does look fantastic, but glories are by their nature transitory and it soon fades. I reef the motor glider round in a fast (for a T-61!) 180 to port, followed by a swift reversal to starboard but it's gone. Because a glory is always centred on the antisolar point (which is, by definition, diametrically opposed to the sun's position in the sky) and below the observer's horizon, they're often a short-lived spectacle. It sure was a good one though, and along with the stunning cloudscape has made this a memorable flight for me, as well as Randa! I fly some more students, but an approaching cold front has made the weak wave system collapse and the drizzle turns slowly but inexorably to rain, wetting wings and misting canopies. We decide that prudence is better than precipitation, and pack up. But what a fab couple of days! The club has made some money, but much more importantly all the students flew, and several have said they'll be back.

And me? Flying above the clouds with Elaina and Randa really was special, and I just hope they enjoyed it as much as I did.

Chapter 8
Slingsby Cadet TX Mk.3

It is quite possible that the T-31 (known within the Services as the Cadet TX Mk.3 or Tandem Tutor),has introduced more Britons to flight than any other British-built aircraft. Why? Well, the RAF took delivery of 131 Cadet TX Mk.3s between 1951 and 1959, and only phased them out around 1986. Most flew more than 25,000 flights each, while one is on record as having logged a staggering 120,000 launches! A simple calculation indicates that just the Air Cadets' TX Mk.3s flew more than three *million* launches, of which the majority were air experience flights. That's a lot of cadets!

It may seem incredible, but it took until 1950 before the British gliding movement finally realised that the solo method of flight training left something to be desired, and that 'something' was considerably fewer accidents! Although intended to produce lots of pilots, the 'solo system' primarily produced lots of broken gliders. The Air Cadets needed a 'cheap 'n' cheerful' two seater, and Slingsby had just the thing; - a tandem two-seat development of the T-8 Tutor, (known by the RAF as the Cadet TX.2) which had in turn been derived from the Kirby Kadet. (The Air Ministry changed the spelling from 'Kadet' to 'Cadet' in 1943, you can probably guess why). The prototype first flew in 1949, with the first production T-31B flying the following year.

The subject of this flight test, was built at Slingsby's Kirbymoorside factory in 1953 as works number 695. It became WT900 when it joined the RAF, and it spent a considerable amount of time with 633VGS at RAF Kinloss. After becoming a civilian machine in 1986 as BGA 3727, it was eventually purchased by Sea King pilot DJ Gibbs, who flew it at the Portsmouth Naval Gliding Club at Lee-on-Solent and then at RAF Cranwell, before both it and DJ joined the recently reinvigorated Buckminster Vintage Glider fleet in 2018. By the time it arrived at Saltby it had logged almost

25,000 launches, and it is a tribute to both the initial design and the construction skills of the men and women who built the aircraft that it still flies today.

As one would expect of such a venerable flying machine, the principal materials used in its construction are the same as those used in the very earliest aeroplanes – wood and fabric. The fuselage is of fabric-covered box girder construction, while the leading edges of the strut-braced wings are covered in plywood and the rest with fabric. Spoilers are fitted to the top of the wing. The large triangular tailplane is also strutted with fabric-covered control surfaces, while the fin is tiny and the rudder huge! There is no trim. An interesting facet of the T-31 is its 'tail ballast' (a substantial weight located on a bracket on top of the tailplane and held in place by a pip-pin). As the aircraft was specifically designed to be soloed from the front (to ease conversion onto the T.8) Slingsby included in the design a quick, easy and safe method of adding additional ballast when flown solo.

The undercarriage is as uncomplicated as the rest of the aircraft, being just a tailskid and large unsprung monowheel mounted behind a nose skid. WT900 has been modified with a small wheel built into the tailskid to aid in ground handling. There are two Ottfur launch hooks; - an aerotow hook set right in the tip of the nose and a CG hook by the mainwheel.

But enough of dry histories and technical specifications, what is this interesting artefact of aviation history like to fly? Well, the key to enjoying a 31 is the same as for most other vintage flying machines - choose your day carefully! Pick the right day and it's great fun, pick the wrong day and it can easily end in tears. More than 15kt straight down the runway and even the ground handling can be fraught, while any appreciable crosswind is asking for trouble. What you want is very little wind on the ground and fat, gentle thermals. So, with that in mind, let's go flying – but first, a word of caution. Ingress – and particularly regarding the rear cockpit – is not easy. When I climbed into WT900 for the first time last summer, it was the first time I'd been in a 31 for 45 years - and although time waits for no one, the weight put on over time is another matter entirely. The cockpit is considerably more snug than I remember. Perhaps unsurprisingly, the field of view from the rear cockpit is rather poor, but from the front it is excellent. Once strapped down by the classic RAF four-point harness let's acquaint ourselves with the controls and instruments and trust me, this won't take long as the cockpits are perfectly in keeping with the rest of the aircraft, being delightfully simple. Each pilot has only a stick, rudder pedals, spoiler lever and cable release knob. Interestingly (and perhaps somewhat surprisingly, as it was intended for cadets) nothing adjusts. A small centre console carries the instrument panel, which is as uncluttered as you would expect. WT900 is as delivered from the factory, and is only fitted with an altimeter, ASI and 'Cosim' variometer. The 'Cosim' is an amusingly archaic device, consisting of red and a green pith pellet in a pair of tapered vertical glass tubes connected to a flask. A perpendicular scale alongside the tubes indicates feet per second, coloured arrows at the base of each tube match the pellets and signify whether you're climbing or descending. It is surprisingly sensitive for such a primitive instrument and watching the different coloured pellets bobbing up and down certainly adds to the charm of flying a T-31, particularly when it is the green one! Anyway, its past lunchtime, so it must be launch time! Now, when Fred Slingsby watched the prototype's maiden flight 70 years ago I doubt he ever imagined that his creation would still be flying in 2019, let alone being aerotowed behind an over-powered ultralight. He designed it to be winch-launched, and to be honest it really isn't pleasant to aerotow.

Once the towrope or winch cable has been cast off, the speed should be above 40 if ridge soaring, and around 35 knots if thermalling. The wing really wasn't built to go fast, but finally and reluctantly stalls at around 28kts solo, and 33 dual. At thermalling speeds the primary controls are all quite light and pleasant, although when the T-31 is being aero-towed they 'firm up' considerably. As mentioned earlier, there is no trim available. One advantage of the very slow speed is it its quite easy to centre in a thermal, the green pellet shoots up the tube and everything is great – and gets even better if an inquisitive buzzard or curious red kite joins you. Like all aircraft that fly *upon* the air rather than *through* it, the sensation of flight is pure and simple, and this is further enhanced by the open cockpit. The aircraft's slow speed and frangible construction creates a feeling of safety and security. Even the very necessary ritual of donning flying suits, gloves, scarves, helmets and goggles adds to the enjoyment of the flight, although the importance of being correctly attired should be obvious. I've always said you should dress for the occasion, and on this occasion, it's going to be cold. But the view more than makes up for it! Being towed up so high for the photoshoot gave me an incredible perspective on a lovely morning. The fantastic view from the front seat was enhanced by the open cockpit, for which I must admit a strong preference. You wouldn't think that the few millimetres of Perspex imposed by an enclosed cockpit would make that much difference, but they do. They make all the difference in the world. The sensation of flight is so much stronger when you can feel, even smell, the air you're flying in. Floating high above the beautiful Vale of Belvoir with just the gentle sigh and sough of the wind in the wires is a visceral, memorable, experience.

Of course, as with most things, all this pleasure does come at a price, and in this case that price is performance – or to be more precise, a distinct lack of it. The best glide ratio of a T-31 is barely 18:1, and this is achieved at only 37 knots. Consequently, even a small headwind has a profoundly detrimental (and to the occupants, profoundly depressing) effect on the aircraft's progress over the ground.

Sooner or later (and its generally sooner) it's time to return to base. After a prudently tight circuit (it is *so* important not to go too far downwind) turn final, extend the spoilers and pitch down for about 45kt. The spoilers are not the most effective airbrakes ever devised, but - if needed -

the T-31 sideslips with ease, charm and grace, while simultaneously sinking like a rock. Rudder it straight, a gentle flare, pause, then sink softly onto the grass. If the landing has been made into a wind of any strength, the ground speed at touchdown is remarkably slow and the ground roll correspondingly short. Upon landing, the pilots' expressions, be they an ab-initio or 1,000-hour veteran are always the same – grinning from ear to ear.

In conclusion, all I can say is that if you want the sensation of flight distilled to just about its purest form (but don't want to use your legs as the undercarriage), then you really need to fly an open cockpit glider!

Chapter 9
Ferry Flight

It was dawn, and in the cold light of a January morning the Black Mountains certainly looked dark and ominous, almost menacing. An icy wind whipped across the airfield, stinging my face with sleet while on the mountain tops the clouds twisted and turned like tortured wraiths. Wisely, I went back to bed.

An hour later though the cloud-capped peaks were a lot less intimidating. The mountains were perceptibly brighter and the sky slowly clearing as I finished my coffee and walked out to the Pawnee waiting patiently in the dull light of a Welsh winters morning. A quick phone call had revealed that the weather at my destination was also improving, so I cranked Piper Pawnee G-AZPA (AKA 'Old Gasper') into life and taxied slowly out to the runway. Gasper was going for its annual inspection and I had therefore spent most of the previous day giving it a thorough clean. Unfortunately, weeks of rain had made the field very muddy and although I taxied very slowly and carefully, anxious to keep it clean, my best efforts were to no avail. As the wheels splashed slowly across the airfield I shook my head ruefully as the propwash picked up some mud and splattered it messily across the gleaming white struts. The field was very muddy. By the time the pre-takeoff checks were completed and the oil was warm the sky was definitely brighter, although the wind had freshened considerably. I swung the Pawnee on to the runway and smoothly opened the throttle.

With a low wing-loading, at least 20kts on the nose and 235 eager horses under the cowling 'Gasper' was off the ground before the throttle reached the stop. A quick beat-up for the benefit of the single other person on the field and I set course for Bidford-on-Avon.

For many modern aviators the prospect of flying a "Day/VFR only" single-seat single piston-engine aircraft around mountains in a British winter would be a little intimidating, and some would feel distinctly uncomfortable without at least a radio and GPS. I am perfectly happy with none of these things, and am content with compass, chart and stopwatch. I know where I am, I know where I'm going and should the weather deteriorate to the point that continued flight becomes unwise I shall simply pick a field and land in it. Something 'Gasper' and I have done many times.

As I cross the border between England and Wales I turn directly downwind and notice a significant improvement in my ground speed. With such a powerful tailwind 'Gasper' is really travelling over the ground, and I rapidly revise my ETA. It's very different from the last time we'd come this way the previous December. That day there'd also been a strong south-westerly wind and – crucially – high pressure.

As I'd suspected a nice lee wave was standing above the Golden Valley, clearly marked by a classic lenticular cloud. The sky has sufficient energy potential to down the most powerful flying machines yet devised, but if the knowledgeable pilot can tap into even a fraction of this potential their efforts will always be rewarded. Drawing nearer the glowing, luminescent cloud I swung my Pawnee to parallel it and was immediately gratified to see the VSI's needle leap to over 2,500ft/min 'Up'. I would like to write a great deal more on the beauty of lenticulars, but it is almost impossible to do them justice. Far better pens than mine have tried and failed. With such a prodigious climb rate the Mogas limiting height was reached within minutes, so I briefly played with the cloud and admired the 'brocken spectre' created by the Pawnee's shadow and surrounded by a beautiful glory, and then reluctantly swung away in a huge sweeping circle and dived towards Bidford. There's no wave today, but the tremendous tailwind and very impressive groundspeed are worthy consolations and we race across the Malverns and continue in a long steady dive, engine roaring.

I soon spot my next waypoint as the aerials at Defford are extremely easy to see, but I search without success for the tethered balloon which the NOTAM says is at Pershore. Defford and Pershore are two enormous ex-RAF fields. Today they are apparently lifeless, how different they must have been fifty years ago, with the serried ranks of fighters and bombers lined up on the apron. Now only the ghosts of the Spitfires and Wellingtons line the deserted giant runways.

I arrive at Bidford in record time, to discover that the replacement Pawnee needs fuel, as it always does, and I exhort the ground crew to "top it right up". Today has been the fastest trip to Bidford I have ever made, and it follows that the return trip will undoubtably be the slowest as it'll be straight into wind. If I have to dodge a few showers as well....

Fuel tank filled, I flick mag and master on, shout "clear prop' and thumb the silver starter button. The big metal propeller rotates slowly and then spins into shimmering life, the airframe shuddering in sympathy. As I wait for the oil pressure to rise I consider how different 'Delta Sierra' (AKA 'Daisy') is to 'Gasper' even though it is the same mark of Pawnee, a 235C. Along with very different wing tips, it has a standard exhaust stack and original two-blade propeller. It is also much noisier, and the cockpit considerably smellier. It probably did more crop spraying. It also has a very lumpy tick-over, although this smooths out when a few revs are added. Daisy flies a lot less than Gasper and it almost seems as if the Pawnee is fidgeting impatiently, eager to be back in the clean sky once more.

At barely half maximum all-up weight and with a very fresh wind on the nose the lightly-loaded tug springs into the sky. Although much noisier than Gasper's four-blade Hoffman prop, Daisy's two-blade McCauley certainly produces more thrust. After takeoff we quickly climb a few thousand feet but at this altitude the windspeed is between 40 and 50kts, practically halving the Pawnee's cruise speed and still-air range. This is no good! As I begin a steady descent an RAF Hercules crosses in front of me, at its nearest maybe half-a-mile in front and 500ft below. As the big four-engine transport pulls away I roll into its 'six' and track it with the Pawnee's long cowling. There's something about flying around in single seat, long-nosed low-wing monoplanes. I can't think what it is! But there's no time for playing. If it's not raining at Talgarth they'll be waiting to launch and at this rate it's going to take long enough to get there as it is, so I descend to around 500ft agl. There's usually some sensation of speed when skimming along low, but today my groundspeed is incredibly slow. In fact it is so slow that cruising so low is not in the least worrying as should the engine fail I could park the Pawnee easily into any of the fields slipping oh-so-slowly under the long nose. We seem to be floating more than flying. The engine growls out its one note song and I fidget impatiently as time ticks remorselessly away on the panel clock. As I parallel a long, straight section of the A4130 I am staggered (and depressed) to see a large white articulated lorry practically holding formation on me. What a headwind! Well, there's nothing more I can do about it, and while I'm going so slowly I might as well take the time to look around and marvel at how much the landscape has changed since I last flew this way on that cold December day. Then the ground had been covered with a thin layer of frost and the landscape had stood out in sharp relief. A full-scale copy of the chart on my knee. But today the recent torrential rain and ensuing floods had rendered much of the area almost unrecognisable and totally different from the map.

Vast lakes had appeared where once there had been fields and the streams and rivers had swelled to proportions far greater than were portrayed on my chart. Ancient castles and modern towns cut off, roads swamped, old stone bridges that now went nowhere. The rain has wreaked havoc. A scan of the panel and I think longingly of the still-far off summer. Lazing in my hammock under the tug's wing. The smell of fresh cut grass mixed with dope, oil and petrol. Leisurely walks through the woods and fields to the pub, confident that not only will someone buy me food and beer but also chauffeur me back to my caravan on the airfield. There are worse ways to spend a summer than flying a tug around the mountains. The big white radomes on the disused airfield of RAF Madley finally appear and move tantalisingly slowly towards me. Even the brooding bulk of the Black Mountains is nearly discernible, although the fact that I know exactly where to look will probably mean I see it before I actually do. Another scan of the panel and my gaze returns to the slowly changing world outside my window. It's strange to think I have landed in several of the fields slipping slowly beneath my wings.

As I neared the dark mass of the Black Mountains I moved my track slightly to the north, to avoid the terrible turbulence that in this wind direction lurks in the lee of the 'Cats Back'. Now I can see the unmistakeable shape of Twmpa, and Hay Common begins to slowly loom in the windscreen; how many times have I towed downed sailplanes off of that! Off to the west is the paddock that I pulled Derek out of in his IS-29, while away in the distance is the field that was invaded by cows as I taxied up to Alastair in his Vega. Alastair had sadly died earlier this year, and for a moment my thoughts become sombre, almost melancholy. Then they are washed away by the thought of him playing the bagpipes from the cockpit of the T-21 as it spiralled down over the airfield and I can't help but grin.

At last I can see Talgarth Airfield, and there are already several sailplanes and their pilots waiting impatiently at the launch point. I stow my chart, cinch up my straps and glance at the rudimentary fuel gauge bobbing beneath its Perspex cover. There's enough fuel for at least half-a-dozen tows, and as I curve onto the base leg I can see canopies opening as pilots begin strapping in. It's time to go to work.

Chapter 10
Consolidated B-24J Liberator

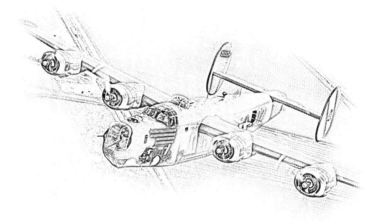

As the P-51 slid into formation with *Witchcraft* I realised just how privileged I was. I was flying a Liberator – the only one currently airworthy – with a fighter escort. I had the yoke in my right hand, the throttles in my left and my feet on the rudder pedals - and as I looked out of my side window across the tops of two huge prop discs a Mustang 'rides shotgun'. What a thrill!

Of course, you don't just jump in a ship (and it *is* a ship) like the Liberator. My introduction to *Witchcraft* had started the day before, when Jim had given me a thorough ground school session on the B-24. Jim is the Collings Foundation's Chief Pilot, and his ready grin and relaxed demeanour hide the fact that he is one of the most experienced – and current – warbird pilots in the world. For example, although he mostly flew the B-17, B-24 and B-25 in 2012, he still also logged around 300hrs in the P-51! He's got a great job. After four hours of ground school Jim left me with a 40-question exam paper on the -24 and said he'd see me tomorrow at 0830.

The next day we completed a comprehensive 'walk-round' and then climbed in through the open bomb bay and up to the cockpit. As you'd expect, it's a very busy cockpit which is dominated by a large console between the two seats. This carries a veritable forest of levers, although my immediate impression was of just how many toggle switches there were - there are literally dozens of them. The centre console carries three sets of four levers. These control (from L to R) the turbochargers, throttles and mixtures, and although the turbocharger and throttle levers work normally, the mixtures are forward for ICO and back for rich. Immediately aft of these levers is a long row of toggle switches that operate the propellers, intercoolers, cowl flaps, pitot heat and emergency hydraulic pump. The prop and cowl flap switches have 'gang bars' which are used when running up, although not in flight. Behind the throttle quadrant is a large box that houses the three trim wheels and more toggle switches, while another box set slightly lower and further back carries various handles and levers that operate the undercarriage, flaps, park brake, control lock and bomb jettison. We were now ready to start the engines, and ran through the 'challenge and response' checklist. Having spent the previous week flying various Rotax 912-powered machines, starting the massive Twin Wasps was a real flight back in time, and here's an interesting factoid – each one of *Witchcraft's* cylinders has almost 1.6 times the cubic capacity of an entire 912, and it has 56 of them! Having checked that the prop arc of engine #3 was clear (this one is always started first as it also powers the hydraulic pump) and that crew chief Whitney was standing by with an extinguisher, I placed my right hand on the correct rotary mag switch (in a row by my right thigh) and turned my attention to the large block of toggle switches by my left knee. These operate the fuel boost and pre-oil pumps, energise and mesh the starters and activate the primers. As each 'Accel', 'Mesh' and 'Primer' toggle switch is for two engines, it is imperative that you know what you're doing! Furthermore, under or over-priming, backfires and a host of other mishandling-related transgressions are treated as 'beer-buying offences' – and *Witchcraft's* crew looked thirsty! Having finished pre-oiling the engine I lifted the appropriate 'Accel' and 'Mesh' toggle switches, waited until six blades had marched past my window, then lifted the 'Primer' switch, counted three more blades and turned #3's mags to 'both'. The engine slowly awoke, smoke streamed back from its exhausts and the prop began to blur as I quickly moved my hand to the mixture lever and gently drew it back into 'Auto rich'. With the engine rumbling happily and the oil pressure steady I began the process of starting #4, having reminded myself that I'd need to press the relevant switches down this time! Eventually all the engines were running smoothly but there's no time to waste, as *Witchcraft* burns around 300lit/hr at tick-over! "Good work Dave" said Jim, adding "now, you reckon you can get this thing out to the runway?" One of the Liberator's many claims to fame is that it was the first heavy bomber to enter production fitted with a tricycle undercarriage, yet the nosewheel of the close-coupled tricycle undercarriage is not steerable and only castors. Jim confirmed that taxying is a bit tricky, as is landing. It is imperative that you don't land on the nosewheel, while care must also be taken to avoid hitting the tail bumper. The mainwheels retract into the wing, and as the wing is mounted quite high on the fuselage the wheels require a long strut which is reinforced with a side brace and forward drag strut. Braking is by hydraulically-actuated expander brakes, two on each wheel. According to Jim the brake pucks are made from a material called 'Unobtanium' – and must be used sparingly and with care.

Having taken a deep breath I sat up straighter in my seat, slid my feet up the rudder pedals, released the parking brake and – with no small sense of occasion – grasped the four throttles. These are the reins of 4,800 horses, which wait to be set loose. In a series of ugly, uncoordinated lurches *Witchcraft* made its unsteady way along the taxiway, and as its nose wandered drunkenly from side to side I felt the first rivulet of sweat run down my back. Out of the corner of my eye I could see Jim struggling to suppress a grin. As I continued to wrestle with this unwieldy beast I knew two things – this was going to be one of the most memorable – and demanding – flights of my life! As I'd suspected, taxying was a real challenge and we initially proceeded along the taxiway in a series of lateral lurches; the expander-type brakes are quite 'grabby' and as the nosewheel isn't steerable it's not easy to keep straight. The trick is to not apply any rudder (so that the pedals remain central) and to keep your feet up on the top of the pedals but only brake lightly and occasionally. God knows what it's like taxying across wind. Furthermore, I was acutely aware of the 33.5m wingspan, and very grateful that crew chief Whitney Coyle was keeping watch from the hatch immediately in front of the top turret, as the field of view is surprisingly poor. Having successfully made it out to the run-up area we commenced the run-up checks. These are numerous and included cycling the electric props from fine through coarse and back while checking that the 'pitch stop' lights illuminate, testing the feathering buttons, magnetos, turbos, cowl flaps and many other items. While using the 'gang bar' to cycle the electric props it was interesting to note the difference in the rate of change, and I was not surprised when Jim reiterated that in flight the props are adjusted individually. Checking and testing the myriad systems took time, and I was slightly embarrassed when the Mustang's pilot (who was behind us) good-naturedly grumbled about the delay, as his engine was becoming uncomfortably warm. Eventually everything was set, and we lurched out onto the runway. Having rolled forwards a couple of metres to ensure that the nosewheel was straight and straddling the centreline, I stood on the brakes and slowly eased the throttles forward until the MP gauges showed 30 inches, then released the brakes and smoothly opened the throttles up to about 40. Leaving Jim to fine-tune the power to 42ins and 2,700rpm I concentrated on keeping straight as the airspeed began to build. The rudders came alive immediately, and as the ASI's needle swung through 65kt I eased the yoke back just enough to lift the nosewheel off the runway. The speed continued to build and at 105 I slightly increased the backpressure, the urgent drumming of the wheels stopped and the big bomber slid into the sky. "Positive rate" said Jim. "Undercarriage up please" I replied while dabbing the brakes to stop the still-spinning wheels. The speed kept increasing and as we passed through 500ft I had a vague guess at easing the power back to Maximum Except Take Off (METO) while Jim raised the flaps from 1/3rd down to up. Just as he'd warned me the Liberator sagged and then sinks momentarily as the Fowler flaps retracted into the wing. At 2,000ft and 130kt I levelled out and re-trimmed while Jim delicately adjusted the power from 'climb' (35"/2,300rpm/'Auto Rich') back to 'cruise' (30"/2,000rpm/'Auto Lean'). Jim primarily controlled the manifold pressure with the turbochargers, as having used the throttles to reduce power to a couple of inches below that required, he then gently added the extra boost with the turbochargers. And even at these parsimonious power settings the four mighty engines were still guzzling around 600lit/hr! With the fuel and hydraulic boost pumps off, cowl flaps set, intercoolers open and all the other details attended too I settled back and tried to get a feel for the Liberator's handling. During the briefing Jim had emphasised that although you need to be this machine's master and not its servant you definitely can't bully it – it's just too big. He'd also explained that it's mostly flown with the elevator trim wheel, and as our excited passengers insisted on walking around inside the cavernous fuselage I soon saw what he meant – I was constantly re-trimming. In fact, the Liberator is very sensitive longitudinally, and it is extremely important that during taxi, takeoff and landing everyone remains seated and that no one is aft of the waist guns or forward of the cockpit. This also explains why the C-87 freighter version was so poorly regarded, for although a bomb load is obviously accurately weighed, concentrated close to the CG and suitably restrained, the same certainly can't be said for a miscellaneous cargo that has been loaded by a tired ground crew. Ernest K. Gann described the C-87 as "an evil bastard contraption" – although as he almost crashed one into the Taj Mahal on takeoff this may well have coloured his opinion! It's also not very speed-stable; if the nose is allowed to drop even slightly below the horizon it accelerates rapidly, and if pitched above the horizon it decelerates just as quickly. I tried some gentle turns and quickly realised it is important to lead with the rudder and that the controls are quite heavy and also not very powerful. This may be because they're all fabric covered. I soon concluded that the indifferent controls, poor longitudinal stability and below-average field of view must've made a heavily-laden Liberator a right pig to fly in formation at high altitude. (When I subsequently discussed the B-24 with famous test pilot 'Winkle' Brown, he opined that the best description of a Liberator was 'lumbering' – although he did allow that it had exceptional range and an excellent autopilot).

The Mustang tucked in tight. One of our passengers was a 90-year old Liberator crewman, and to see the 'little friend' sitting just off our starboard wing must have been a very emotional moment for him. On the way to our destination of Zephyr Hills we made a small diversion to fly over the famous 'Fantasy of Flight' – and this gave me another opportunity to assess the handling, for as the people on the ground heard the rumble of our engines and looked skyward Jim suggested I fly a couple of reasonably tight turns overhead to "wake Kermit up". Zephyr Hills appeared far too soon for me, and having completed the pre-landing checklist with the props at 2,000rpm and between 25-27ins MP I concentrated extremely hard on keep the speed and altitude nailed as we turned downwind. Jim is an excellent instructor, and just gave me gentle prompts such as "here's about right for the first stage of flap" and "I usually drop the gear about now" or "try about 24 inches and 2,000rpm. You want 130mph on base". I gave myself a generous downwind leg and a wide base, and as the Liberator settled onto final I was immensely gratified to see that (thanks to Jim's excellent coaching) the speed and glideslope were bang on. The rest of the flap went down and I gently juggled the throttles to keep the speed steady at 105kt as we flashed over the fence. Easing back on the yoke I slowly drew the power off and tried to maintain the right attitude. The undercarriage is quite close coupled, and although I needed to avoid touching the tail bumper (another beer-buying offence) it's imperative to land on the mainwheels and hold the nosewheel off. The wheels touched fractionally sooner than I'd planned, but the touchdown was reasonably smooth and – remembering those 'Unobtanium' brake pucks - I held the nose up for aerodynamic braking. The runway is about 1,500m long and I knew that Jim expected me to use it all, as long as the last 150m is at a slow speed. The runway is free, but brakes and tyres are expensive (and that's if you can even find some!) As the speed diminished I lowered the nosewheel and just *thought* about braking. The brakes are powerful, and if applied firmly they'll certainly stop the wheels, although the tyres may continue to revolve. This probably constitutes a brewery-buying offence! Once clear of the runway we raised the flaps, pushed the mixtures back into 'Auto Lean', then opened the cowl flaps and bomb bay doors. "Great job Dave" grinned Jim, before adding "you can start breathing again now!" Emboldened by Jim's praise I taxyed confidently back towards the large crowd waiting at the other end of the airfield for the 'Wings of Freedom' tour. The B-17, B-24 and P-51 will visit over a hundred cities as they tour the US in 2013, and be seen by literally hundreds of thousands of people. Would this many people go to see some dusty, lifeless machines in a museum? I very much doubt it. But the superb spectacle of these magnificent machines roaring through the overhead has drawn a large crowd, all eager to see some living history.

Once safely chocked, I regretfully eased the mixture levers forward into ICO, and as the muted thunder of our mighty engines died away and the giant propellers slowed to a stop I was filled with tremendous respect for the brave men – many of them practically still boys – who flew the Liberator against flak and fighters in the death-filled skies of the Second World War.

Chapter 11
Snakes & Dreadnoughts

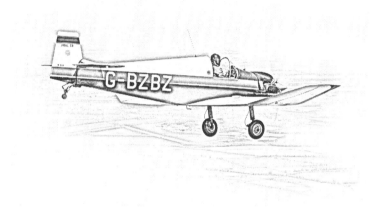

Why do you fly? I suspect that the answers are as varied and disparate as any group of aviators. Many fly for fun, some for pay and quite a few for both. For me, one of the greatest attractions of being airborne is basically, the view. The ability to simply see further really is as good a reason as any to get airborne, and in the Spring and Autumn the light can have an extra special quality. Incredibly, you can still meet people who, having conveniently forgotten all about the Southern Hemisphere, think that the winter is a product of the Earth being at the furthest point in its orbit from the Sun or aphelion, around the winter solstice, when in fact aphelion occurs in July. In fact, the Earth is at its nearest point - perihelion - in January. Seasons are of course all about the Earth's tilt, and if you live anywhere between 30 to 60° north or south of the equator the sunlight, which is already more precious in winter due to its scarcity, can create almost magical illusions due to the way the sun's rays hit the atmosphere. There isn't room here to discuss phenomena such as Mie scattering and Rayleigh scattering, but throw in some freakishly long shadows and sharp contrasts with both accentuated by the lack of foliage, and some truly amazing sights can be seen. For example, I was airborne early in the morning on a clear crisp day recently, and the visibility was so good that I could almost see tomorrow. What I could see was three large power stations billowing out great clouds of smoke and steam, which were drifting downwind on a brisk breeze. I've been flying around this part of England for almost 20 years and had never seen it before, but the incredible illusion was of several gargantuan dreadnoughts all steaming westwards across a weird green sea. It looked amazing.

Similarly, I was flying east in the afternoon a week or so later and saw a sight that genuinely made me do a cartoon-like doubletake. Suddenly I spotted what looked like a huge silver snake slithering southwards at tremendous speed across the fields, and just for a second sat bolt upright in the cockpit and thought "what on *earth* is that?" Then I realised it was a train. The stretch of the East Coast mainline just south of Grantham is extremely straight (it is where the Mallard set the still-unbroken speed record for a steam locomotive) and in places slightly elevated. Some very weird optics and atmospherics created by a combination of the low sun in the west and the train's direction of travel (essentially perpendicular to the sun's rays) had contrived to turn each bare metal coach and its windows into mirrors, creating the illusion of an enormous shiny, speedy serpent. I am very aware that the description of both these remarkable sights simply doesn't do them justice, but they really were quite extraordinary.

Truly, winter aviating can be spectacular and a day recently was just made for it! A cold front had gone through overnight, leaving a chill, crisp mid-winter morning. I just had to fly! As many of the trees had lost their leaves and most of the shrubbery and undergrowth had died back the fields and towns stood out in sharp relief, while the lack of foliage alongside the canals, rivers, roads and railways made the map strapped to my knee much easier to interpret. For example, the section of Ermine Street, the old Roman road from London to Lincoln south of Grantham and known as the high Dike is obvious, as are all the disused railway lines and abandoned air force bases that proliferate around here. Another advantage about flying in the winter is that the cloud tops are generally lower, and as I take an almost perverse delight in flying high above the clouds in an open cockpit I climb my little Jodel above the dazzlingly white clouds into the ice-cold blue. For cold it undoubtably is, despite my multiple layers. But it's a good kind of cold, I imagine the Victorians probably would have called it 'bracing' - and mostly I'm reasonably snug except once when I stretched slightly and my head just protruded above the windscreen. Then I got a blast of freezing air down my back through the tiny gap between my leather helmet and flying suit, and it is as shocking as if someone had poured ice water down my neck. It really makes me gasp. That'll teach me to forget my silk scarf! Back on the ground I think about the previous hour. It was a tremendously enjoyable flight, filled with beauty and wonder, and just to round it off four F-15s roared through the overhead as I climbed out of Buzz's tiny cockpit. The Eagles look magnificent, and as they disappear into the distance on their way back to Lakenheath I wonder if they even saw my diminutive Bebé on its short grass strip. I've often ruminated how - as well as being a science, aviating is also an art, which may explain why flight in any of its myriad forms exercises a fascination that is both hard to explain and difficult to resist. The F-15 Eagle drivers have their pressurised cockpits and high-pressure flight plans, while I simply sit behind a sheet of Perspex and glance at a chart occasionally. In truth, it's hard to imagine more dissimilar single seaters than a D.9 and an F-15, yet they both fly. And on a day like today, what else do you need?

Chapter 12
Focke-Wulf Fw-44 Stieglitz

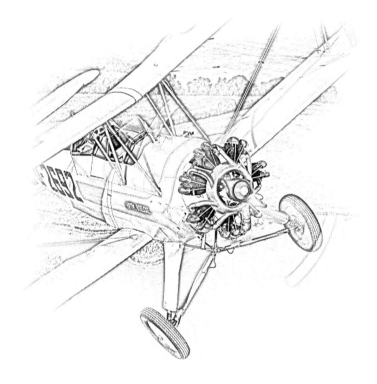

It's certainly fair to say that the Focke-Wulf Fw44 Stieglitz (German for 'Goldfinch') is a pretty rare bird. Indeed, the example standing in front of me on that warm autumn afternoon at Old Warden was the only one I'd ever seen, and is the first on the UK register. My initial impression was that it closely resembled a 7/8ths scale Stearman, but without the brutish charm of the big Boeing biplane. Somehow the Stieglitz just appeared more stylish and sophisticated – 'European' if you will. That said, it does look rather more rugged than its contemporary, the elegant Bucker Jungmann.

The Fw 44 is a single-bay biplane and I noted that both sets of wings have identical span and a very subtle sweepback, with just a slight stagger. Both the top and bottom planes also have a small amount of dihedral, but what really got my attention is that there are ailerons on both the upper and lower wings. Peter had already enthused about the sparkling roll rate, and I began to look forward to the forthcoming flight with excited anticipation.

As I began to move around the Focke-Wulf I could clearly see that it had been designed with typically Teutonic thoroughness. It was also interesting to note that the various servicing hatches for the fuel and oil were colour coded, and this is carried over into the cockpit. Although common today, this was innovative stuff in the 1940s and in fact it was the Germans who invented colour coding.

The engine is a Siemens 'Bramo' SH14A-A4 seven-cylinder air-cooled radial, which produces up to 160hp at 2,200rpm. It turns a wooden Hoffmann two-blade fixed pitch prop, and is fed by a pair of fuselage-mounted tanks with a combined capacity of 135 litres.

The methods and materials used in the construction of the Stieglitz are an interesting mixture. The fuselage is a welded steel-tube lattice structure with wooden stringers, while the wings are made of laminated pine and plywood. The undercarriage was particularly noteworthy, as the large fully-castoring tailwheel didn't look quite 'right'. Furthermore, I'd also noticed the big handles set immediately in front of the tailwheel and surmised (correctly) that this machine had originally been fitted with a tailskid.

Overall, I really liked the look of it – with one glaring exception. As mentioned earlier, I'd already ascertained that this machine was originally fitted with a tailskid, and that its substitution with a fully-castoring tailwheel was unlikely to have improved the ground handling – and in particular its directional stability during the landing roll. I made a mental note to be extra careful when landing, particularly as there was very little wind, which meant that the rudder would be relatively ineffective at the end of the ground roll.

Access to either cockpit is excellent. There are doors on both sides, and well-located grab handles. A first-rate feature is the data panel incorporated in the left side pilot's door. This shows the weight & balance schedules, recommended speeds as well as the engine and airframe limitations. During the preflight walk round I had been amazed at the extraordinary attention to detail, and this had certainly been maintained in the cockpit. It is simply stunning. The seat adjusting mechanism is very neat - you just twist the top of the lever to unlock it, and then raise or lower it to adjust the seat. The panel is very nicely laid out (although I'd prefer the ASI to be where the clock is), and has luxurious leather trim on the doors and cockpit coaming. All the controls fall easily to hand, with the only ergonomic aberration being that the pitch trim wheel is on the right side. This, of course means you must change hands on the stick when trimming.

As mentioned earlier, the Germans invented colour coding, and not only are the ASI and engine instruments colour-coded, but so are some of the controls. For example, the knob on the fuel selector lever is yellow while the oil shut-off valve is brown. I also noted that all of the instruments (except the altimeter, due to UK certification requirements) are metric.

Starting just about any aero-engine of this vintage is something of a ritual, and as we prepared to bring the big 'Bramo' to life Peter introduced me to something that I'd never seen before. The engine primer has its own separate reservoir, which is actually inside the cockpit. This must be filled before trying to start the engine. Then I unscrewed the locking collar on the primer plunger and squirted fuel into the cylinders as Peter pulled the prop through. It fired up first swing, and showing a fair degree of possibly misplaced trust, Peter sat in the front. This was remarkably brave of him as there are no brakes in the front cockpit, and I'd already ascertained that it was at the end of the ground roll when you'd need them, as the rudder would become ineffective.

Taxying out revealed that the forward visibility really was quite good for a biplane of this vintage, although I wasn't particularly enamoured of the brakes. The geometry of the rudder pedals is such that you really have to point your toes to make the hydraulic drum brakes work. Furthermore, they are not very progressive, and tend to be either all or nothing – with very little feel or finesse. While writing up this report, I'd spoken to the doyen of test pilots, Captain Eric 'Winkle' Brown, who flew literally dozens of captured 1940s German aircraft during the Second World War. He told me that – with very few exceptions – German aeroplanes were almost always cursed with unsatisfactory brakes. As the Germans clearly possessed some of the finest engineers in the world, neither of us could explain why they seemed incapable of designing decent brakes. However, Eric felt that as the Luftwaffe operated primarily from grass airfields, that this could have had an influence.

With the uncomplicated pre-take off checks concluded, I lined up on runway 03 and slowly opened the throttle. Acceleration was good, and I experienced no difficulty in keeping straight. The elevator became effective almost immediately, and I gently picked up the tail, greatly enhancing the view forward. I anticipated a slight swing as the tail came up, but the Stieglitz ran straight and true as the airspeed rose. As noted earlier, the ASI is metric, although I will use knots. I gently eased back on the stick at about 55kt, and the Stieglitz lifted off gracefully after a ground run of around 250m. The data panel incorporated in the left side pilot's door recommended 110km/h (60kt) as Vy, but on Peter's recommendation I trimmed for 120 (65kt) for better forward visibility. G-STIG is not fitted with a VSI, but I would guess that our rate of climb was somewhere around

600fpm, as we reached 1,000ft AGL in a little under two minutes.

My initial impression was that the directional stability was somewhat 'soft'. Indeed, the slip ball was all over the place, and Peter laughingly pointed out over the intercom that he knew I was slipping and skidding as the wind in the wires was practically singing! In fact, the powerful rudder is remarkably light and sensitive and it took me a while to master it. Apart from this, I was extremely impressed almost immediately. The spacious cockpit is comfortable and (for a biplane) the visibility good. The engine is responsive and the ailerons remarkably authoritative! They really are excellent, granting the Stieglitz a tremendous rate of roll. For a biplane of this era, control around the longitudinal axis is truly exceptional, and it has easily the most efficacious ailerons of any aeroplane in its class. The elevator is also well balanced and powerful. In fact, I'll stick my neck out here and say that the Stieglitz is the best handling World War Two basic trainer that I've flown – and I've flown almost all of them... including the Magister, Tiger Moth, PT-22, Stearman and Jungmann. That said, harmony of control isn't perfect, as the rudder seemed a little too light, at least initially.

I always like to ascertain how an aircraft handles on the slow side of the speed scale, so as soon as we had climbed to a safe altitude I began decelerating for an examination of the stall. This proved to be very innocuous. Indeed, if the speed was reduced at a steady 1 knot per second – with the slip ball centred and the nose just above the horizon – there wasn't really what I would call a classic stall. Instead, the Stieglitz simply sank straight ahead with gentle airframe buffet and a high sink rate at about 38-40kt. A more vigorous approach, with the nose held way above the horizon and the speed reduced more quickly, provoked it into reluctantly dropping its nose and a wing. Recovery was easy and immediate, merely release the backpressure and the Stieglitz was flying again.

Accelerating out of the final stall, I set the power to the cruise rpm of 1,950. This produced about 90kt, for a fuel flow of around 40lit/hr.

Back in the circuit at Old Warden I noted from the appearance of the very lethargic windsock that the gentle zephyr still favoured runway 03. I would've liked a bit more headwind; particularly as 03 has a slight downslope. Peter recommended that I use 120 'kippers' (kph and about 65kt) on final, but I came over the displaced threshold about five 'kippers' too fast. Usually just being only 2-3 knots over Vref wouldn't matter, especially in a draggy old biplane. However, the combination of a warm day, very little headwind and a downward-sloping runway resulted in a protracted float. Consequently, although the three-point touchdown was very smooth, it was a good way into the field. As Peter had predicted, at the very end of the ground roll it tried to swap ends, and only a deft dab of right brake prevented a ground loop.

After another easy takeoff my second circuit was better, as I turned in earlier. The angles and speeds seemed OK all the way round, yet somehow I still appeared to float a bit before another smooth touchdown. Once again it tried to chase its own tail, and Peter warned me against even thinking about attempting a relatively high speed turn off as we lurched towards the taxi way. (To tell the truth, all I was doing was trying to keep straight!) There was no doubt in my mind that it would be a lot easier with a tailskid, as it would have scored (both literally and figuratively). Once a skid has dug into the ground it really does slow you down, as well as help keep you straight.

Peter then dismounted, and - as is often the case with a machine like the Stieglitz, it's easier solo. You've got a much better view and a greatly improved power-to-weight ratio. I made a textbook takeoff, and as I rolled into a smoothly banked turn and glanced at the instrument panel I was gratified to see that the ball was right in the centre.

I've written before that formation work really shows up how well an aircraft flies – and the Stieglitz did not disappoint. For a 1930's aeroplane the handling is nothing short of amazing. The motor is powerful and the elevator authoritative, the rudder responsive, and as for the ailerons, they really are exceptional. This machine is wonderful to fly.

Back in the circuit, I was determined to get it right. Ignoring the displaced threshold (which does produce a rather odd picture) I concentrated on the numbers, and as I drew abeam them I slowly closed the throttle, wound the elevator trim all the way back and banked towards the runway into a classic curved approach. The needle of the ASI was glued to the 120 mark, and as soon as my aiming point started to move up the windscreen I squeezed on just a suggestion of power, and then almost immediately pinched it off again. Despite my best efforts, it still seemed to float briefly as I came over the numbers. With practice, I think that 110km/h would be a perfectly reasonable approach speed in calm conditions, although of course 03 does have a slight downslope, which would exacerbate the tendency to float.

The touchdown was a smooth three-pointer but, as anticipated, at the very end of the ground roll it did try to swing. However, I was used to its foibles by then, and a swift stab of right brake soon showed it who was in charge. Having carefully taxied back in, I let the engine idle for a few minutes to allow the Ts and Ps to stabilise. This gave me the ideal opportunity to ponder on the previous 45 minutes.

In conclusion, the Stieglitz immensely impressed me. It is a very handsome flying machine with – for the 1930's – incredibly crisp controls. The handling really is excellent, and the only facet that I didn't like was the castoring tailwheel, which has blighted it with a propensity for trying to ground loop at the end of the ground roll. And of course, this is not how Kurt Tank designed it. The advantages of a tailskid when landing are two-fold. Not only is some of the braking force being applied behind the CG, but it also improves the directional stability. So, in light of all the above, why is the Fw 44 so rare, when there are so many Jungmanns about? I think there are two reasons. The Focke-Wulf factory was probably busy producing '190s, and I suspect that most of the surviving Jungmanns were built in Spain by CASA. One thing is irrefutable – some of the greatest pilots of the World War Two flew with the Luftwaffe – and that's not surprising when they learnt on a trainer as good as this.

Eventually I shut down, climbed out and walked over to where Peter was waiting with a big grin on his face. "Well..." he said, "what do you think?" "It's absolutely fantastic," I replied, "it goes even better solo, and that odd, intermittent whining noise that I occasionally heard over the intercom has also gone away." Peter's brow furrowed in puzzlement, and then he grinned broadly. "Cheeky," he laughed.

Chapter 13
Skiing in Bumblemunk

Hoorah! We're back out of lockdown, I draw back the curtains and see that the sky is an ice-cold blue. Perfect. I've been cooped up in a socially-distanced TV studio for the last few days, and although it's been good fun I'm eager to get off the ground. Chipmunk Mk.23 *Bumblemunk* needs some exercise, the engine barks into life and the wheels are soon crunching through the thin layer of snow that covers the airfield.
As soon as the oil is warm I slide the canopy closed, line up and open the

throttle wide. The engine roars out a joyous challenge to the waiting sky as it sucks in great gulps of oxygen and the propeller is taking big bites out of the thick, cold air with every revolution. It really does seem as if *Bumblemunk* and I share the same urgency to slip gravity's 'surly bonds'. Climbing out over the Vale of Belvoir with the Lycoming pulling like a locomotive the snow-covered landscape is really pretty and the visibility phenomenal. It seems like I can almost see next week. It's a great day to fly, and I've got a plan. Like far too many of us, my great friends Mike and Lisa have suffered loss and sadness recently, and as it's Lisa's birthday she deserves a flypast. So just before takeoff I texted them to go into their garden at 12.15. They live right on the edge of their village, and by careful planning I make several wing-waggling fly-bys and steep reversals over the nearby fields without breaking any rules. Now what? On an impulse I push open the throttle, pull back on the stick and *Bumblemunk* roars skyward, engine singing. It's amazing how pure and clean a fresh covering of snow makes everything look, and I can feel my spirit soaring along with the needle of the VSI. From 4,000ft Rutland Water stands out like a great blob of molten gold, while the snow blanket seems centred on Saltby. Perhaps a couple of big 360s are in order, and I swing *Bumblemunk* across the unsullied sky in a great sweeping arc. The air is like glass, and I allow myself a smug smirk of satisfaction when a brief buffet confirms we've hit our own wake. I really don't want to land, but I'm only supposed to be exercising *Bumblemunk* as owner Richard is otherwise engaged, and as I want to do a couple of circuits reluctantly head back. The first landing is decent enough, but the less said about the second one the better! I'm not finishing on a thumper like that, and I've an idea. I don't usually bother with pre-setting the brakes, but this time apply two clicks on the downwind leg and flare with just a dribble of power on. Success! As I'd hoped, the sink rate on touchdown is so slight that for a magic moment the wheels are skiing across the snow. The tyres literally aren't turning as there's no weight on them and we're sliding sensuously for several seconds. Then the wing passes the weight to the wheels, they sink through the snow, the oleo struts compress and the Chipmunk slows quickly to a stop.

I could've quit there, but take up the offer of flying the last tow of the day, so I'll be landing long. The sailplane's crew are practicing a medium-level cable break and on the base leg a glance in the mirror confirms their radio call that - as briefed –

they'll be landing long on the grass 07, while I'll go for the tarmac 07. The EuroFox has quite a strong pitch-couple with full flap, and as I want to try and ski again deliberately set only 1/3rd flap and leave some power on. Settled on final and starting to slow down I sense movement in my peripheral vision, and there's the K-21 off the starboard wing, exactly where I expected it to be. It belatedly occurs to me that we should've got someone to video it, because for a few seconds it must've looked great with the glider and tug seemingly wingtip to wingtip and quite close to the ground. Even the light (an orange winter sun, low on the horizon) was perfect. Driving away through the gathering gloom I'm well chuffed – and I know I'm not the only one, judging by all the smiling faces as we pack the hangar. News of a breakthrough with a vaccine has really lifted everyone spirits, as has the sheer poetry of flying over the snowy landscape on a sunny day. The forecast isn't overly encouraging (it is December after all) but judging by the number of beautiful photographs posted on the Buckminster GCs Facebook page that evening everyone's got some great memories to tide them over till the next good flying day. And me? The sweetness of that last landing in *Bumblemunk* still hasn't worn off as I write up my logbook that evening. I've mentioned before about the simple pleasure that can be had from the subtle and seamless transference of weight from wing to wheel, and when you get it right and literally 'ski' onto snow its especially 'subtle and seamless', with an extra soupcon of smoothness for good measure. Magic!

Chapter 14
The Tow Must Go On

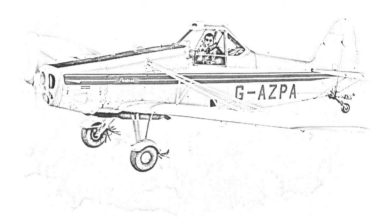

Ah, tow business – there's nothing quite like it. The roar of the engine, the smell of the crowd! It was 07.30 on Monday morning, Day Three of the task week, and the view of the airfield from my caravan window was certainly encouraging. A thin patina of frost glistening on the wings of the sailplanes waiting in the crisp May morning indicated that the night time temperature had been unseasonably low, while the cloudless sky promised a warm day. Perfect gliding weather! Consequently, inside the clubhouse long cross-country flights were already being planned, declarations photographed and barographs prepared in anticipation of a good, and possibly great, day's gliding.

The resident sheep were already (and somewhat reluctantly) being ushered off the field – clearly, someone had decided that it was high time to "get the flock out of there!" Other club members were removing the collapsible fence at the end of the main runway and unpacking the hangar, while at least a dozen gliders were being rigged, fettled and their ballast tanks filled with water in expectation of strong soaring conditions. I knew I was the only tug pilot on site and it was becoming increasingly obvious that if I didn't put in an appearance soon, they'd come looking for me. Shrugging on my tattered old flying suit, I headed out in search of coffee and, if I was really lucky, a bacon butty.

Two cups of coffee and a pre-flight later I climbed into Piper Pawnee *'Gasper'*. Our trusty tug coughed quickly into life and I taxied out to run-up the engine in preparation for the first launch. While I waited for the oil temperature to rise off the stop I admired the lovely morning light playing across the Black Mountains and thought once again how lucky I was to live and fly in such a beautiful place.

The first pilot had declared a 750km triangle and had briefed me quite comprehensively as he required quite an exact profile for his launch. He wanted to be just west of the airfield at 4,270ft QNH on a northeasterly heading and at his sailplane's Vt (maximum aerotow speed). As a tug pilot, it is important to try to provide the tow you've been asked for, as 750km is a long distance without an engine and it is always helpful if the glider gets off to a good start. At 10.06 hrs we were at 4,270ft, with 106kts on the ASI, just west of the airfield and heading 045°. He released and streaked off towards the cumulus that were already beginning to form over England while I spiralled back down towards the airfield for a look at the windsock.

The windsock indicated a very gentle northerly wind, so landing uphill to the east looked best. Having landed, I let the roll-out carry me back towards the next sailplane waiting at the start of the downhill north-west runway. Throughout the day the preferred choice for takeoff remained the northwest runway, with landings to the east, although if a glider were in the way I would occasionally land on the southwest runway or launch towards the west. Typically, the glider pilots insisted on landing all ways, even southeast! At first, this may sound confusing and even outside the realm of normal airfield operating procedures. The reason lies in the nature of Talgarth airfield, which is quite small, dome-shaped and situated midway between a river valley and a mountain range.

As the airfield is not overly large, best use must be made of the down slope when taking off and landing, while being so close to the mountains can produce some very strange conditions. For instance, on days when an east wave has formed, the upper wind can be howling from the east at near-gale force, yet the combination will launch into a gentle west wind. This is formed by the airflow reversing near the surface, due to the 'rotor' created by the wave, and is a potential trap for the unwary – woe betide any pilot who (as they've always been taught to do) tries to land into wind on this occasion.

The small size of the airfield and the unusual conditions produced by its close proximity to the mountains are just two aspects of Talgarth that make tugging here so interesting. And as the day wore on and the tows mounted, I thought of another – the tremendous variety of sailplanes that are sometimes launched.

Indeed, at 12.18 after a morning of launching fast 'glass ships', towing the venerable Slingsby T-21 was a world apart. It meant going from flying as fast as I could to as slow as I dared! While the combination was still at quite a low altitude, the antique T-21's equally ancient pilot meandered hopelessly out of position and yawed the tug badly. I didn't enjoy that launch much, as introducing an excessive amount of yaw while flying just above the stall at low-level isn't likely to be habit-forming.

After lunch I launched the day's first visitor, a Schleicher ASW-20 from Sleap in Shropshire. However, as I descended towards the threshold of 09, a less welcome visitor casually drove across the runway. I had been watching the car all the time – nevertheless it made me think that I really should do something about improving the warning signs at the gate.

Having got the ASW-20 safely on its way, a lull in the launch rate gave me the chance to grab a coffee, chat to some of the 'spotters', and try to talk them into having a trial lesson.

Taking time to chat to prospective punters often highlights some very amusing, if not understandable, misconceptions. For example, most are quite surprised that the two-seater will land them back on the field. Presumably they think gliders simply drift downwind like a balloon. Others are relieved to learn that an instructor will fly with them! I'm sure most of them don't believe me when I tell them sailplanes have flown distances of more than 2,000km and climbed to nearly 50,000ft.

That afternoon a Schemp-Hirth Cirrus from Bidford in Warwickshire arrived, again on the southwest runway, despite the tug and most Talgarth-based gliders landing to the east. With everyone landing in different directions and few calling their circuit, it certainly kept me on my toes. Indeed, it well behoves the 'tuggie' who aspires to a long life to keep a good look-out, both on the ground and in the air. On some days there can be as many as 20 gliders flying the same short ridge beat, and they all expect the tug to give way.

At 15.42, off the top of a launch, I spotted the IAR-Brasov IS-32 landing on Rhos Fawr common. After a quick call to Talgarth base to send a car and tow rope, I curved down towards the grounded glider. There's something about a field retrieve that always makes me sit up a bit straighter in the cockpit. Each one is different and there are many factors to consider before even attempting a landing, let alone a takeoff. Indeed, on some occasions simply finding the glider can be quite difficult, but on this occasion the retrieve was completed without incident.

After 30 or so tows my hammock beckoned beguilingly, but at 17.30 a Schleicher K-23 from the Long Mynd in Shropshire came in, followed promptly by news that our LET L-13 Blanik had landed on Hay common. Having assured the Blanik's pilots that I'd pick them up on my way back from Shropshire, I refuelled both the tug and myself and we set off on the long tow back to the Mynd. It was a lovely evening, with outstanding visibility. The patchwork fields basked peacefully in the evening sun as the combination climbed slowly north, the Pawnee purring like a contented cat. After such a busy day, it was very pleasant to simply sit back and enjoy the beauty of flight, especially over such spectacular scenery. As we climbed slowly northwards I found myself singing away and mangling the immortal lyrics of Irving Berlin's classic song "There's No Business Like Show Business". "Yesterday they told you would not go far, then they gave you a Pawnee and there you are, on the hangar door next day they've hung a star, so let's get on with the tow! So let's get on with the toooowwww!" Then the appalling thought hit me that if the PTT switch was jammed on (as can occasionally happen) I'd just treated every glider pilot within radio range to some truly ghastly singing!

As we passed overhead Hay, I could see the Blanik's metal fuselage glinting in the evening sun and pinpointed its position.

Once the K-23 had released near the Long Mynd, I reefed the tug round in a steep 180° turn and slid swiftly earthwards while thinking about my second field retrieve of the day. Mind you, Hay common is so big it barely counts as a field retrieve, and another advantage as far as I was concerned was that I had already landed on it this year. However, despite its size, the common is still fraught with traps for the unwary as the surface is strewn with rocks, some quite large. Reminding myself of this, I vowed to drop the rope and then over-fly the intended landing area, just as I would for every other field retrieve. There is no place for complacency in any area of aviation – an observation doubly true when landing in an unprepared field! As I drew nearer I could see several microlights parked near the glider, and assumed that their pilots had landed to have a look at the Blanik. This was good news, as it meant I could ask one of them to attach the towrope to the sailplane and run with its wing. Having dropped the rope I landed, taxied up to the Blanik and hopped out to ask the microlight pilots for some help. The microlight pilots were amenable to my suggestion, and even sportingly helped push the glider to a better position. Having admired the microlights, thanked their pilots for their help and shown one of them where to attach the tow rope I climbed back into '*Gasper*', cranked it into life and taxied into position for takeoff.

All went well, and we launched off the common at 18.24. The Blanik released at 1700ft and soared back down the ridge while I flew home for my 36th and final landing of the day.

I taxied briskly towards the hangar, cut the engine and coasted slowly onto the hard stand. A dab of left brake and the Pawnee pivoted neatly in front of the hangar, perfectly positioned to push back. "Aren't you going to reverse it in then?" asked someone sarcastically. There's no pleasing some people!

Once the fence had been re-erected and the sheep let back out, I trudged wearily back to my place, but it was the same sad 'tuggie's' caravan story. I'd got lots of bottles but no food, so I was forced to go to the pub, where they have both. Whilst waiting for my lift to the pub I sipped a single bourbon, watched the sunset, and looked forward to doing it all again the next day.

It's true, there really is no business like tow business – well, no business I know.

Chapter 15
North American T-6

The North American T-6 (more correctly known as the AT-6, for Advanced Trainer) is a truly iconic aircraft, and also my type of machine! Consequently, when the opportunity arose to fly one with Warbird Adventures (probably the world's most experienced T-6 outfit) – well, I didn't need asking twice! I'd flown a T-6 a couple of times previously, but this time it would be with Warbird Adventures' owner Thom Richard, at the company's then-base at Kissimmee, Florida. Our aircraft, N451WA (call sign 'Texan One') is actually an ex-US Navy SNJ and was built by North American Aviation at its Dallas, Texas factory in 1945. It's interesting how modern its systems are, bearing in mind that the prototype first flew in 1935. Indeed, when it was first introduced into RAF service in 1938 it was the most modern aircraft in the RAF's inventory, significantly more sophisticated than a Spitfire or Hurricane. For example, it has a powerful, supercharged engine turning a constant-speed propeller, and an engine-driven hydraulic system to power the undercarriage and flaps. Furthermore, the flaps can be set to any position you like (up to a maximum of 40°). By contrast, the Spitfire Mk.I had a hydraulic system driven by hand-pump, pneumatic flaps that were only either 'up' or 'down', and a crude, two-position prop. The T-6 also had a fully enclosed cockpit, blind flying instruments and ample electrical power, enabling it to be fitted with internal and external lighting, radio communication and navigation equipment comparable with contemporary operational aircraft. Finally, and perhaps most importantly, the relatively high-wing loading meant that it had similar handling characteristics to the Spitfire and Hurricane.

As I moved around the aircraft, another thing that struck me was its size. It stands over 3.5 metres tall and weighs in at over 2,400kg. It really is quite large for a two-seater, and if your usual mount is a Cessna or Piper, it may well appear quite intimidating. Its sheer size, combined with the military paint scheme and pugnacious round nose certainly does give it a wilful, belligerent appearance – indeed, as I gazed up at it I could almost imagine that it was looking back at me with a slightly disdainful air, as if almost daring me to see if I could master it. As I was soon to discover, it will 'bite' if mishandled, though to fly it well is a reward in itself.

The heart of all powered aircraft is the engine, and the T-6's is a beauty. Lurking, half-hidden, under the cowling is one of the world's greatest aero-engines – the immortal Pratt & Whitney Wasp. This air-cooled nine-cylinder radial has a swept volume of 22 litres, and puts out its 600 horses at 2,250rpm and 36 inches of manifold pressure. If you're finding the concept of a 22-litre engine a bit difficult, consider this – each one of its nine cylinders has more than twice the swept volume of the entire engine of most cars! The undercarriage is blessed with a reasonably wide track, as it retracts inwards, and it is notable that the wheel brakes are hydraulic (and even better, toe-operated. The tailwheel does not retract, but it is steerable 15° either side of neutral through the rudder pedals. Pushing the stick fully forward unlocks it and allows it to castor. It's a bit of a climb up to the front cockpit but the well-designed handholds and steps ensure that it is not too onerous; although I'm sure it must have been a lot harder with a heavy old seat-type parachute. The tall stick is topped with a pistol grip, and as my forefinger curled around the trigger I noted the armament selector panels. With switches for 'Cowl Gun' and 'Wing Gun', 'Right Bomb Rack' and 'Left Bomb Rack', as well as a pair of safety switches marked 'Fire' and 'Safe', I could almost smell the stench of cordite mingling with the heady aroma of AvGas and oil. Because, make no mistake, the T-6 is undoubtedly a warbird, and one with a very impressive combat record. I couldn't help wondering what it must have been like for the USAF pilots who flew Texans in their daily duels with the flak gunners over the 38th Parallel in Korea and above the Ho Chi Minh trail in Vietnam, or for the RAF pilots flying Harvards during the Mau Mau uprising in Kenya.

I soon began to feel quite comfortable in the cockpit. Although at first glance it looks a bit cluttered, closer inspection reveals that it is reasonably well-designed, with the various systems and sub-systems all laid out logically. The instrument layout isn't brilliant, but it isn't bad either – with one glaring exception. The fuel tank gauges are mounted in the floor! This design feature has probably caused more than a few accidents, because although the maximum fuel capacity is 420 litres, the rate at which it is consumed varies widely. For example, with the power at METO (Maximum Except Take Off – 32.5in MP and 2,200rpm) it's a very thirsty 212lit/hr. However, pull the power right back to the best economy setting of 20in MP and 1,600rpm and the fuel consumption drops to around 85lit/hr. One particular anomaly is the 'power-push' for the hydraulics. This is a large yellow knob next to the flap and undercarriage levers, which when pressed builds up pressure in the hydraulic system for between 45 seconds to two minutes. The hydraulic pump is on all the time, but when the 'power-push' is actuated, the system temporarily builds up pressure by restricting the return flow. When it is not engaged, the system free-flows. The 'power-push' must be pressed before operating either the flaps or the undercarriage. Sensibly, the brakes are on a separate system.

Outboard of the flap and undercarriage levers is the large rotary fuel cock and immediately in front of that are a pair of large hand wheels. These operate the elevator and rudder trims, with the elevator being inboard. Both handwheels have a small notch cut into them, and the relevant trim setting is at 'neutral' with the notch in the '12 'o' clock' position.

Time to wake the Wasp. As the propeller began slowly to revolve, a ribbon of smoke curled lazily backwards from the exhaust and with a series of coughs and grunts, the enormous engine growled into life. As the pulse of the motor began to throb through the airframe it really did feel like a huge animal was coming to life. Starting an engine like the Wasp is an experience in itself, and if you have any mechanical soul at all I guarantee you'll revel in the wonderful, liquid rumble of that big round engine.

With the massive motor grumbling quietly to itself and the temperatures and pressures all satisfactory, it was time to taxi out. Although there a strong temptation to wave (there's bound to be a few folk watching) it's much more important to weave. That curvaceous cowling blocks a significant amount of the view forward, and it is imperative to proceed along the taxiway in a series of sedate S-turns.

Pre-take-off checks include cycling the prop at 1,600rpm, checking the mags, mixture and manifold pressure at 2,000rpm and then testing and locking the carb heat, before pulling the throttle right back to check the idle rpm, operating the 'power push' and noting the hydraulic pressure. Other checks include ensuring that the fuel is on either 'Reserve' or 'Right'. The 'left' setting is not used for takeoff as it draws from a stand-pipe in the left tank which only allows access to 133 of the 209 litres total capacity in that tank. The 'left reserve' setting feeds from the bottom of the tank, which gives you access to the entire tank capacity. The 'right' feeds from the bottom of the right tank. The idea was for students to use the right and left up first and if the engine then quit, they still had enough in the reserve (76 litres) to make it home. Unsurprisingly, this has caused a lot of confusion and accidents over the years, since the 'left' selection is not the entire left tank.

The flaps are left 'Up' (except in the case of a short field take-off) while the trim wheels are set to around 10-11 o'clock for the elevator and between 1-2 o'clock for the rudder. Incidentally, when checking the rudder for full, free and correct, it is important that the tailwheel is unlocked.

I taxied slowly into position and lined up – taking care to ensure that the tailwheel was straight. There's a lot of metal whirling around up front, and when all 600 horses start pulling there is a distinct tendency to swing to port. It is definitely advisable to make sure you're pointing in the right direction at the start. Under Thom's careful tutelage I slowly opened the throttle. Full power generates a lot of noise – and I can honestly say I didn't notice at all! I really was concentrating hard as we accelerated. As I picked the tailwheel up there was a slight swing, but I caught it with the rudder, then eased back on the stick and we rose into the air. So far so good, but I fumbled for the power-push and it took a couple of extra seconds before I got the wheels up.

My initial impressions of the T-6 as a fine flying machine were soon confirmed. All the primary controls are powerful and well-harmonised, and any loads on the stick and rudder are easily trimmed out. Visibility is excellent and the engine responsive, but perhaps most of all, this is an aircraft that really 'talks to you'. If you fly slowly, all the cues are there that the aircraft really isn't happy, and if you fly fast the controls soon firm up, while the noise of the airflow almost makes the ASI superfluous. I know it's a bit of a cliché, but the T-6 is a real pilot's aeroplane.

Talking of slow flight, an examination of the stall characteristics was particularly interesting. If the slip ball is out to the right there is plenty of pre-stall buffet as the speed is reduced, but if the ball is (correctly) in the centre there is hardly any pre-stall buffet. This has got a lot of pilots into trouble over the years, since the only real warning before the stall is that the backpressure on the stick reduces slightly.

The actual stall is quite abrupt, and usually produced a vigorous right wing drop as well. On the plus side, recovery was equally quick – simply reduce the backpressure. Annoyingly, on my first couple of stall recoveries I applied some negative 'g', which resulted in the engine coughing and spluttering. I would probably have been a bit more concerned about this if I'd seen the long tongue of flame that unrolled from the exhaust and licked greedily along the side of the fuselage! (I only saw this on the video taken from the wing-mounted camera after we'd landed). Incidentally, the onboard video cameras that record the entire flight are a real asset, and great for the debrief.

Having got the hang of recovering from a stall without the engine coughing in protest, I moved on to some basic aerobatic manoeuvres.

Having climbed swiftly back up to 5,000ft, I set the throttle to 30 inches of manifold pressure with the rpm at 1,900. The T-6 is a delight to aerobat, although – unlike modern competition aerobatic aircraft – its size and weight mean that things happen quite slowly. I used around 160kt for a loop and 130 for a roll, and was pleasantly surprised at how well they worked out. Rolls to the left are easier, due to that immense radial having some quite powerful gyroscopic tendencies. After a few more chandelles and wing-overs, Thom suggested that we'd better be getting back if I wanted to try my hand at a few circuits. The brief transit back to Kissimmee gave me the opportunity to look at the cruise performance and stick-free stability. The normal cruise power setting is 26in MP with the rpm between 1,800 and 1,850, and this gave us an IAS of 120kt for a fuel flow of around 120lit/hr. Incidentally, when descending care must be taken not to pull the power too far back, as the air should never be allowed to drive the prop of a radial. It is simpler to point the nose down and accept the speed. As we approached Kissimmee, I levelled out at the circuit height of 1,000ft, entered the downwind leg at 45° and slowly eased the power back to 20in MP and 1,800rpm. As the speed dropped below 130kt, I fumbled for the 'power push' and then lowered the undercarriage, before reducing power to 15 inches. The wheels locked down, the speeds and angles all looked about right and I felt that it was all coming together nicely. Another fumble for the 'power push', then full flaps, prop forward both trim wheels set to 9 'o'clock.

Unfortunately, we had to do a 360° on base leg for spacing, and this disturbed my planned approach. And, as we all know – good landings come from good approaches. As we turned onto final power, back and in we went. I managed to hold a steady 85kt all the way in and although the landing wasn't bad, I knew could do better. Having braked gently to a stop I taxied back to the runway for another go. This time it was much better. I didn't fumble for the 'power push', speeds and power settings were more precise and the smooth landing generated a rare compliment from Thom. One more equally good circuit and reasonable landing and another memorable flight was in the logbook.

In closing, I can clearly see how the T-6 earned the nickname 'Pilot Maker'. With its advanced systems, powerful engine and high-wing loading, it was clearly the ideal training aircraft for pilots who were going to fly Spitfires, Mustangs or Corsairs, as its handling characteristics were so similar. Furthermore, it is also obvious why it is still so popular today – it just oozes charisma!

Chapter 16
An Interesting Day

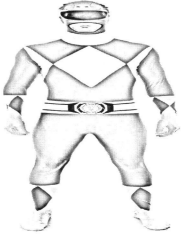

"What on earth is that thing?" We're passing through 3,000ft in a strong thermal, nearing cloud base and closing rapidly on a true Unidentified Flying Object. Initially I'd thought it was a big bird marking a thermal, then a bunch of helium-filled party balloons tied together and now I don't know what to think. Hesitantly, my passenger Mark ventures an opinion. "I..I think" he stutters tentatively "I think it's a man!" The sunlight catches it as I bank closer and the hairs on the back of my neck suddenly stand up. It is a man!

The day had started reasonably normally. I was duty tug pilot at the Buckminster GC, and along with flying the tug a rather interesting task was scheduled for the day. Fellow tug pilot Al Munro had recently joined the vintage group with the express purpose of flying the group's Slingsby T.31B Tandem Tutor, and for a very simple reason. His first solo had been in a Cadet TX Mark 3 (as the RAF called them) in 1958. The plan was I'd check Al out and then, all being well, send him off; - 60 years to the day since his first solo, in the same type! And this presented me with an interesting conundrum. Not only had Al, quite literally, been flying before I was born, but his well-worn logbook evinced some interesting types. His first operational tour had been on the Gloster Javelin, and subsequently he'd been a pilot (and latterly an instructor) on both the mighty Phantom and the Tornado, before moving on to flying A320s for the airlines. However, even with (or perhaps because) of his vast depth of experience, Al knows that 'currency counts', and I'm a lot more current on the T.31 than he is. So, *quod erat demonstrandum*, I am P1. The weather is perfect (6-8kt, straight down the centreline) the glider serviceable and Al and I are giggling like a couple of little kids as we position the venerable sailplane on the runway. But, as Robert Burns observed in 'To a Mouse' "the best-laid schemes o' mice an' men gang aft agley" – and the principal reason why our "best-laid scheme" had "gang aft agley" was that - like most of us - Al is no longer the fit, agile and supple young lad he'd been back then. It rapidly became apparent that he wasn't going to fit in the front without major surgery. The 'go solo' plan has - quite literally - failed to get off the ground, but Al is determined to fly in a T.31 on his anniversary so (with a considerable amount of swearing, laughing, manipulation, and at one point a rather worrying "Shit – I'm stuck!") we succeed in wedging him into the rear cockpit. The aerotow goes well until we hit a strong thermal at about 300ft, ensuring that the next 30 seconds are best described as 'sporting', but eventually we release in lift, soar for a while and then return safely. Curiously, his egress – while still problematic – is a lot easier than his ingress, and we share a heartfelt handshake by the cockpit. "Well Al" I grin "Happy Diamond Solo Anniversary - we did it!" "Indeed we did" he laughs "and we must never do it again!" A few hours and several tows as tug pilot later, I'm now in the back of a K-21, flying a Trial Lesson and being towed by Al in the EuroFox. The lift is broken and not easy to work, but about 500 metres to the north-east what looks like a large bird is about 500ft above us, so I head that way. The variometer bleeps its approval and we're soon climbing strongly towards something, but what? We draw closer and the picture becomes clearer. It isn't a bird, and it isn't a plane but, for several unnerving seconds, it is unquestionably a man! My mind reels as I swing the K-21 nearer. It isn't a hang glider, paraglider or parachutist – it's a man, about my height and build, and seemingly suspended in space, 3,000ft above the Vale of Belvoir. "Could he be wearing a jetpack?" asks my passenger, disbelievingly. I knew that the JB11 JetPack was flown at the Goodwood Festival of Speed recently, and that it could climb this high. But......"It can't be!" I reply. And it isn't. I warily circle around the thing and eventually draw the conclusion that its almost certainly some sort of helium-filled balloon in the shape of a super-hero, possibly Spider-Man, maybe Iron Man or perhaps a Power Ranger. I'm not sure, but one thing I do know – it is surreal. It has obviously attained neutral buoyancy and is at the mercy of the thermals, so for several minutes we circle it while Mark takes pictures. However, the south-westerly wind is carrying both it and us away from the airfield, so with discretion being the better part of valour we leave it to its own devices and head for home. Back on the ground Mark and I babble excitedly to the ground crew. "You won't believe what we've just seen" we tell everyone within earshot. I've done a bit of flying, and seen some amazing sights from some equally impressive cockpits, but the moment when I honestly thought I was looking at a man who could fly and the hairs on the back of my neck stood up will take some beating. So yes, it was an interesting day.

Chapter 17
SZD-45A Ogar

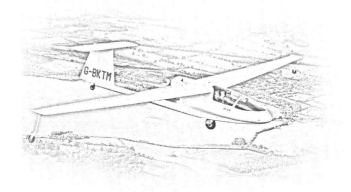

As we float serenely across Rutland Water I glance across at Roger Pitman and grin wryly. "You weren't joking were you Roger? It really does look like you're sitting in a deckchair!" "Well, might as well be comfortable!" he laughs in reply. I don't just enjoy the quantity and quality of the aircraft I'm lucky enough to test, but also the variety. Some aircraft display almost national and cultural idiosyncrasies (such as the difference in handling between American and French four-seaters), and others even their manufacturers' political ideology. Conceived in the depths of the Cold War the SZD-45 Ogar (Hound) is a fascinating flying machine that I've long wanted to fly. It is also one of the most unusual-looking aircraft ever made. While waiting patiently at Saltby airfield for it to arrive we all heard it before we saw it. And when we did see it we knew what it was, because it looks like nothing else! Featuring a pod and boom configuration, a high-wing, T-tail and powered by an engine mounted at the back of the fuselage that turns a pusher propeller, it both looks and sounds unmistakeable.

As it taxis towards me I can't help but think how ungainly it looks, with one wingtip-mounted outrigger firmly on the ground and the other pointing at the sky. Then I realise that as the other wing really is a long way off the ground it would actually be easier to taxi than a T-61 or RF-5, as you don't need such a wide taxiway! While I'm still processing this, it pulls onto the grass and performs a very deft 180 turn, in not much more than its own length! Anyone who's ever flown a T-61 or RF-5 will know why I put an exclamation mark at the end of the preceding sentence. It might look a little clunky on the ground, but looks aren't everything. The prop stops and the large aft-hinged canopy swings open and back. I can see Roger unstrapping and preparing to disembark, then realise that the cockpit sills are extraordinarily high off the ground. For the life of me I can't see how he's going to get out – and more importantly, how I'm going to get in. Suddenly, he produces a set of welded metal steps, which he carefully places on the sill and then climbs out. Amazing! One thing is already irrefutable, the Ogar is full of surprises! And as I begin to inspect it in greater detail the surprises just keep coming. Some aircraft are made from metal, others composites or wood; well, the Ogar uses all of them.

The engine is mounted at the rear of the fuselage pod, aft of the wing's trailing edge, and at the same level. It is a Limbach SL1700EC air-cooled flat-four derived from the classic VW 'Beetle', and produces 68hp at 3300rpm. It is fed from a single fuel tank of only 30 litres directly behind the cockpit and turns a two-blade composite pusher propeller. Access to the engine is excellent. There's several inspection panels in the cowling, while the entire top half opens like a car bonnet.

The monowheel undercarriage consists of a mainwheel fitted with a cable-actuated drum brake, outrigger wheels mounted on flexible struts right out at the wing-tips and a steerable tailwheel. The mainwheel is mechanically retracted into the fuselage, but in common with many motor gliders (and some other Soviet-era aircraft such as the Yak-52) it only half-retracts. The upside of this design is that should you land wheel-up (either by accident, design or malfunction) no damage is done. The downside is that it doesn't reduce total drag by that much. The tailwheel steering unit is supported by a phosphor-bronze bush which Roger describes as "a work of art, and almost as expensive!" I was already starting to get the impression that the Ogar had been built to a specification, not a price, and part of the plan was to make lots of work for lots of people. It's very well made, albeit somewhat over-engineered. In another significant difference between capitalist and communist thinking, not only do the wings not fold, but I got the distinct impression that de-rigging would not be a trivial affair, and would require the assistance of several comrades! What really impressed me though was the quality of the workmanship. It is beautifully made.

Access to the cockpit is unusual. As mentioned earlier, as the sills are very high it carries its own detachable step. This system was a first for me and may even be unique.

The canopy opens wide and is held open by well-damped gas struts, and the cockpit big and comfortable, while as the sticks and seats are slightly staggered the cockpit feels even wider as you're not constantly rubbing shoulders with the other occupant. Roger puts his seat right back, the pedals right forward and it looks like he's sitting in a deckchair!

Settling onto the comfortable seat I like the uncluttered look of the instrument panel, which is as wide as the cockpit and has all the instruments laid out in a single row. There are inherent cooling problems with air-cooled engines in a pusher installation, and I wasn't surprised to see that the CHT gauge is disproportionately large.....

The engine started promptly and rather nosily, although I hadn't really expected anything less as the engine is mounted up high on the wing to allow a low undercarriage while still providing good prop clearance. An inevitable consequence of this type of engine installation is that it will be inescapably noisy. Firstly, you have an air-cooled engine situated quite close to your ears, and secondly, as with all pusher-type installations the exhaust pipes are unavoidably mounted in front of the propeller disc, meaning that the exhaust is discharged into the prop, which chops it up, creating more noise.

Taxying out revealed, for a monowheel, good characteristics. The suspension seemed reasonably well damped, the brake adequate and the tailwheel steering powerful and precise, as the turning circle is impressively small. With an outrigger on the ground the cockpit is well canted over, but I soon get used to it.

The POH emphasises that the stick should be fully forward at the start of the takeoff roll, something I would strongly advise against in most monowheels, because as soon as the tailwheel lifts you (A) lose tailwheel steering and (B) there's a strong tendency to yaw, due to the propeller. However, as the Ogar has its centre of thrust quite close to the centre of gravity and centre of pressure this isn't an issue. It took a while before the elevator bit and could lift the tailwheel left the ground; conversely, the ailerons come alive almost immediately, making it easy to balance on the monowheel. Incidentally, another inherent disadvantage of pushers is that when taking off or landing in rain there isn't any propwash to clear the water off the windscreen. I keep the Ogar balanced on the monowheel as the speed builds, then a hint of back pressure and it waffles into the sky at about 45kt. I hold the aircraft in ground effect until we have another ten knots then ease into a shallow climb. Bearing in mind the Limbach is some 50% more powerful than the Stark-Stamo and the performance is still far from startling, the prototype must've been distinctly marginal. The climb rate isn't bad. Initially I wasn't overwhelmed, until I realised the VSI was under-reading, but it's certainly noisy (both in the cockpit and as I noted when Roger departed – from the ground). The CHT's stayed within limits, but a long, slow climb would be inadvisable.

The regular crew of Al and Keith in the BGC EuroFox are already on station above the photogenic Rutland Water, and as Keith's door pops open I slide into formation with confidence. As we sail above Rutland Water it suddenly occurs to me that the Ogar's pod and boom design is somewhat reminiscent of a Republic SeaBee, and that with its boat-like hull and pronounced keel it'd probably ditch well. The cockpit is also very comfortable, and I wonder if SZD had their eye on the export market, as the comfy seats seem more suitable for the bourgeoisie than the proletariat!

With all the photos in the can I start my examination of the general control and stability characteristics. I paid particular attention to changes in pitch trim with power, because a well-known side effect of high-mounted pushers is that the high thrust line produces significant changes in pitch whenever the throttle is adjusted. On the Ogar this effect seemed negligible, and easily trimmed out. It's a very stable aircraft, and the controls are adequate, although harmony less so. The stick is quite short and the heavy ailerons need a firm hand at speed, while the elevator is quite light. The rudder is powerful, breakout forces reasonable. The rate of roll is acceptable and visibility in the turn (and indeed every phase of flight) is truly excellent. An examination of the stick-free stability confirmed my original assessment; it was designed as a trainer and the emphasis is much more on stability than control. A ten-knot displacement from a trimmed speed of 60kt produced a low amplitude long wavelength phugoid that eventually damped itself out after several lazy oscillations. Directional stability is softly positive (unsurprising, as the pod-and–boom means there's lots of keel forward of the centre of pressure, despite the large fin), and spiral stability just barely neutral. As you'd expect with any motor glider, the slow-speed characteristics are very benign, and it just sort of mushes and wallows as the stall is approached, before the wing finally quits at about 38kt. The pre-stall buffet was negligible and recovery quick and easy, with minimal height loss. It stalls in the same way it does everything else, slow and friendly. It is approved for spins and basic aerobatics, but as its 45 years old I think it would be undignified to treat such a graceful old lady in this fashion.

Setting the throttle to 2,800rpm produces an IAS of around 65kt at 3,000ft, for a TAS of 71. Increase the power to 3000rpm and it slowly accelerates to 70, for a TAS of 76 while burning around nine litres an hour. If you're interested in an old-school air-miles per gallon number, it's around 40MPG. Not bad, which is just as well as the single thirty litre tank means you've only got six and a half gallons to begin with.

Even though the day was rather flat, with very little evidence of vertical air movement, I simply can't wait to turn the engine off, so as soon as we were within easy gliding range of Saltby (just in case the engine didn't re-start) I reduce the power to 2,200 rpm for two minutes to allow engine temperatures to stabilise and trim for 55kt. Then its power to 'flight idle', mags off and slowly decelerate until the propeller stops turning at around 45.

It has been my experience that the wing loading of many modern motor gliders means that speeds above 55kt are necessary to retain sufficient control authority, which makes it difficult to stay centred in an average British thermal. However, the Ogar will thermal quite comfortably at 50kt and as we slid earthwards towards the pre-briefed engine restart height of 1,500ft I finally find a small thermal and scrape back up to 2,000. Great fun. It really is an easy machine to soar, rather like a K-13. The book clams a best glide of 27:1@55kt, which felt about right, while the min sink is quoted at 190ft/min@40kt. This may be slightly optimistic. After an enjoyable 30 minutes of defying gravity by using my intellect as the engine and the atmosphere for fuel I restart the engine and join the circuit.

I find it easier to extend the undercarriage than retract it, and then briefly open the airbrakes to ascertain their effectiveness. They are certainly very powerful, and I quickly stow them until final. On the approach I trim for 60 with the throttle set to idle and control the glide path with the airbrakes. Landing on the grass with a gentle crosswind is easy, the trick is to just ease the airbrakes in slightly as you flare, and aim to touch the tailwheel and mainwheel simultaneously. Pop the brakes back out when you're down and you'll stay down. I would not recommend attempting a landing with full airbrake, as the sink rate is eye-wateringly high and you'll land with the wheel brake on. Narrow tarmac runways and a strong gusty crosswind is a combination best avoided if laundry bills are to be kept to a minimum!

I was very taken with the Ogar, and in my opinion there is no comparison with its closest capitalist counterpart, the T-61. The Ogar is superior in every respect. It's a shame the wings don't fold, (but neither do the T-61s) but you could have a lot of fun with an Ogar exploring wave systems, sea breeze fronts and shearlines, and also hills and ridges that simply aren't accessible by pure gliders.

As I climbed out Keith and Al came over, and both seemed curiously animated. "You should see that thing in flight" enthused Keith "it looks amazing!" Al nodded enthusiastically in agreement. Ogar is Polish for 'Hound' but I can't help but wonder if perhaps Łabędź (Swan) would've been more apposite. It may be a bit of an ugly duckling on the ground, but it is very much an elegant swan in the sky.

Chapter 18
Percival Pembroke C.1

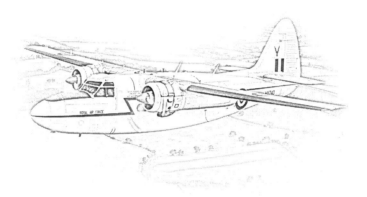

As we wandered out to the Percival Pembroke called *Percy*, my initial impression was that it really is quite a large aeroplane. I'd spent the evening before studying the *Pilot's Notes*, but although I knew that it had a MAUW of over 6,000kg, for some reason it still looked bigger than I'd expected!

During the pre-flight briefing *Percy's* owner Martin Willing had mentioned that this is very much a pneumatic aeroplane, so as soon as we made our way to the cockpit one of the first things we did was to check the air pressure gauge located on the co-pilot's sill panel. Ominously, its needle was lolling lazily around the 'zero' mark. Not a good start! However, the highly efficient boys of the Aircraft Restoration Company very quickly diagnosed that a pipe had split in the starboard undercarriage bay, and one new length of pipe and a tank full of air later we were back in business! As Martin had flown the Pembroke into Duxford from Jersey earlier that morning we didn't need to pull the engines through, so we rapidly completed the pre-flight inspection and then returned to the cockpit.

To enable me to fully appreciate savouring *Percy*, Martin had very generously offered me the left-hand seat, as only this side of the panel contains the flying instruments. Indeed, Martin was clearly determined that I was going to get the full Pembroke piloting experience, and indicated that he would only read the checklist, leaving me to action the various items. That this was really going to be a flight back in time became apparent to me as soon as I'd adjusted the rudder pedals and secured my harness. It has been my experience when flying other aircraft of this vintage that they are usually ergonomic nightmares, and in this respect the Pembroke did not disappoint. There are switches, buttons and levers everywhere! In front, above you, on either side, even behind you!

As we continued preparations to 'start engines', I became increasingly conscious that this machine really is a piece of history. As you may have already gathered, starting it is very much a ritual, with a great number of buttons, switches, knobs and levers to be pushed, pulled, twisted, turned and set. Eventually I had everything set satisfactorily. Martin recommended using about three seconds of primer, so having primed the port engine and cracked the throttle open about an inch, I was finally ready. With no small sense of occasion, I reached above my head and opened the little flap that guards the booster-coil and starter buttons. A shout of "clear prop" and I pressed both buttons firmly. The big prop began to revolve and after several blades had scythed past my window, a couple of cylinders fired, stumbled, and then fired again. The propeller dissolved into a shimmering blur as all nine cylinders awoke with a gratifyingly deep radial rumble, accompanied by a big cloud of smoke. As the two-pointer rpm gauge came alive, I released the starter button but continued to depress the booster-coil button until the rpm had increased to 900. I then released the booster-coil button and gently eased the throttle forward until the rpm stabilised at 1,200. The second engine started equally easily, and once both engines were stabilised at 1,200rpm, Martin asked me to turn on the stand-by inverter and check for a white 'dolls-eye'. Having ascertained that the stand-by inverter was functioning normally, I turned on the main inverter, and watched the 'dolls-eye' turn black. While the engines slowly warmed up, Martin directed me to turn on all the radio equipment and conclude the 'post start' checks. As soon as the oil temperature had reached 20°C and the cylinder head temperatures were above 100°C, I checked for a mag drop and also a 'dead cut' at 1,200rpm. Martin then pronounced himself satisfied with *Percy's* performance thus far, and directed me to commence what I already knew was going to be possibly the most demanding part of the flight – taxying! For a relatively large aircraft, the Pembroke is unusual in that it does not have nosewheel steering. Consequently, steering is by differential braking. While this in itself should not really be construed as a source of potential problems, the pneumatic braking system certainly can be!

One final check;- ensure that the nosewheel centring lever on the control column was in the 'Out' (down) position and engaged in the control yoke groove. This is vital as it to enables the nosewheel to castor freely. I then released the parking brake, added a hint of power to nudge Percy onto the taxiway and then as soon as we were rolling on the tarmac immediately drew the throttles back and carefully set exactly 1,200rpm on each engine. This is important, as even a suggestion of differential thrust will make taxying more difficult, and I was already finding it far from easy! Martin had indicated during the briefing that the Pembroke required a certain knack to taxy, and he clearly wasn't joking. Basically, to turn the aircraft in the desired direction you press the appropriate rudder pedal and then squeeze the brake lever on the control yoke, releasing it and applying a small amount of opposite brake as you approach the direction in which you would like the aircraft to move. Other points to remember are that for periods of extended taxying in a straight line it is advisable to have the nosewheel centring lever in the IN (up) position. This applies friction to the nosewheel leg and helps to prevent the nosewheel shimmying – I imagine it is somewhat similar to the friction damper fitted to many older motorcycles. Finally, in order to stop the aircraft in a straight line, it is essential to ensure that the rudder pedals are in the central position before applying the brake lever.

My initial attempts to keep the aircraft in the centre of the taxiway were rather risible, and we proceeded in a rather ungainly sequence of side-to-side lurches. This was accompanied by a constant series of loud hisses from the pneumatic brakes, interspersed with curses from me and chuckles from Martin. He also proffered constant encouragement and advice, while keeping a wary eye on the pneumatic system's pressure gauge. This is very important, as with the engines loafing along at 1,200rpm the engine-driven compressor wasn't replenishing the pneumatic accumulator as fast as I was using the air. The Pembroke was easily the largest aircraft that I'd ever taxied with a castoring nosewheel at that time, and as with many other aircraft fitted with this system it's easier if you don't taxy too slowly – although, of course, it is imperative not to taxy too fast!

Eventually I started to get the hang of it, and as we rolled along a sizeable crowd of museum visitors enjoying the unseasonably sunny weather all turned around on hearing the wonderful rumble of a pair of big radials. The unusual sight of an airworthy Pembroke instantly produced lots of cameras, and I must admit that I did feel a hell of a fellow and gave them a cheery wave as we trundled past.

For the run-up, I pointed the Pembroke into wind, set the braking brake and ran through the pre-take off checks. Although there is a 'Take Off' setting for the slotted flaps we left them at 'Up', as this gives better climb performance in the event of an engine failure, and then reviewed the actual takeoff. The 'engine out' safety speed (Vmc, or 'blue line' speed) with flaps at 'T/O' or 'Up' is 90kt. Consequently, Vr (the speed at which the aircraft is rotated) is always 90, regardless of weight.

The takeoff brief included the procedures to be adopted in the event of an engine failure both before and after 90 knots had been attained. An ex-RAF and Cathay Pacific Captain, Martin definitely falls within the category of 'Master Airman' and the briefing was, as you'd expect, both succinct and comprehensive.

All checks and briefing complete, Martin deftly lined us up (he really did make it look easy) and then reminded me to pull the yoke right back to engage the nosewheel steering damper. A final 'full and free' check of the controls and we were ready to roll, so Martin then uttered those magic words "you have control." Very conscious of being entrusted with a rare piece of the UK's aviation heritage, I smoothly and gently eased the throttles of the two Alvis Leonides up to 40 inches of manifold pressure. Incidentally, it seemed to me that the throttles move over a huge range! I led slightly with the starboard throttle to cancel out any tendency to swing, but the Pembroke ran straight and true. To be honest, this was a relief, as I had not been looking forward to having to use the dreaded differential braking to control the takeoff run! *Percy* commenced his charge down the runway with plenty of noise – and surprisingly good acceleration. However, to be fair, we were several thousand pounds below MAUW. Maximum power is achieved at 46 inches of manifold pressure and 3,000rpm, but *Percy* isn't getting any younger so in deference to his age Martin said that we'd use no more than 40 inches and 2,800 rpm. As the needle of the ASI started to move I relinquished the throttle levers and left them to Martin to fine tune, then placed both my hands on the yoke and, with my feet resting lightly on the rudder pedals, concentrated on keeping straight. As the airspeed continued to build, the rudder came alive, and 90kt came up amazingly quickly. I gently eased the yoke back a surprisingly long way, the nose slowly pitched up to 5° and then, when *Percy* decided that he was ready to fly, we flew!

During the briefing Martin had mentioned that as the main undercarriage legs retract backwards, they shift the CG aft and consequently produce a noticeable nose-up change in pitch trim. Forewarned is forearmed, and as the last of the runway slipped under the nose I squeezed the brake lever and indicated to Martin to raise the undercarriage. As the wheels retracted, I checked forward on the yoke slightly to stop the nose from rising, before giving the pedestal mounted trim wheel a deft roll forward. Although Vy is 105kt, Martin had briefed me to attain 120 before commencing the climb, as this not only provides better visibility over the nose but also produces better engine cooling. As we climbed away at 120, I drew the props slowly back to 2,600rpm before reducing manifold pressure to 36 inches. Even while we'd been taxying out I'd already ascertained that conditions were far from ideal, and as we powered upwards it became increasingly apparent that it really was a murky old day – in fact, only just VFR. Usually I wouldn't fly an air test on an unfamiliar type in such conditions, but with some aircraft you simply must grab the opportunity when it's presented, as it's just too good to miss. We climbed rapidly up to 4,000ft, found a nice big blue hole and I reduced power further and re-trimmed before exploring the Pembroke's general handling. Initially I tried a couple of standard rate turns before trying my hand with some steeper ones. In complete contrast to its porcine and slightly ponderous appearance, I thought it flew like a much lighter aeroplane than it really is.

A look at the slow side of the flight envelope was particularly illuminating, as I was astonished at just how slowly it would fly. Even with the flaps up I got the speed down to 80kt, while with full flap, the undercarriage down and a dribble of power, it almost seemed to be hanging in the air as the ASI needle sank slowly down and almost off the scale to a remarkable 55kt. Interestingly, there was very little aerodynamic buffet as the stall was approached; instead a gentle fore and aft pitching motion developed a few knots prior to the stall. This continued until the nose dropped gently, confirming my earlier impressions that *Percy* really is a very nice, honest old aeroplane. He is also a very solid, stable old bus. Indeed, the only trim I adjusted was pitch, and I never touched either aileron or rudder trim for the whole flight. I suppose you really could describe him as a 'gentleman's aeronautical carriage'!

Accelerating out of the final stall I retracted the undercarriage and flaps while Martin turned off the fuel pumps, set the air intake filter to 'Normal' and closed the oil cooler shutters. With the throttles set for 30ins MP, I drew the props down to 2,500rpm and re-trimmed. Martin said that these settings usually returned about 140kt IAS, which he has found to be the Pembroke's most economical cruising speed. All too soon it was time to go home, but before we did Martin insisted on not only demonstrating, but also letting me fly a couple of graceful chandelles, one of the manoeuvres he often uses at air shows. These really were great fun, although perhaps poor old photographer Duncan sitting back in the passenger cabin might beg to differ!

As we commenced the descent, Martin directed me to switch on the fuel boost pumps, open the oil cooler shutters and then select the air intake filter to 'Filter'. I then levelled off at 1,000ft, reduced speed to 120kt, and pushed the props up to 2,600rpm. Sliding back into the Duxford circuit, I noted that the viz below the inversion was still very poor, and my reduced view of the runway was exacerbated by the fact that we were flying right-hand circuits and I was in the left-hand seat! Once we were established on the downwind leg I called for the first stage of flap. However, Martin reminded me of the Pembroke's dependency on its single pneumatic system (which not only operates the brakes, undercarriage and flaps but even the autopilot) and recommended that, contrary to the Pilot's Notes, I should lower the undercarriage first. If the pneumatics are a bit out of puff he'd rather have the wheels than the flaps, and who can blame him? Indeed, having so many of the services driven pneumatically is possibly the Pembroke's weak spot, which is probably why it never really made it as a multi-engine trainer. A series of circuits really cane the system! Incidentally, despite the noticeable nose-up change in pitch trim as the undercarriage retracts, I don't recall a nose-down trim change as the undercarriage extends. However, you certainly know that it is extended, as a clearly perceptible 'clunk' is felt through the airframe as the legs lock down.

As we were downwind right-hand for 06 Martin called my base and I banked the Pembroke around to fly a constant curve onto final while keeping the airspeed between 100 and 105. At 800ft I called for full flap while pushing the props up to 2,800rpm. Over the fence at 95, squeeze the throttles closed and just hold it off. Not a bad landing at all! Flaps up, throttles up (in fact almost too much power, but the ever-vigilant Martin caught me before I could over-boost the engines) and we raced back down the runway and up into the air. The second circuit was broadly similar to the first, although I drew the throttles too far back on base and Martin called for "a big handful of power" as we went a bit flat. The landing wasn't bad, and I think Martin could see that I was getting ever closer to a real greaser, which is not easy in a Pembroke. Despite the fact that Pembroke tyres are as rare as rocking horse poo, Martin very generously offered me one more circuit. Off we went again, but this time we left the wheels down to give the pneumatics a chance to get their breath back. This time I felt I was really starting to get the hang of it, and there was considerably less prompting from Martin. I pinched some power off on base, then squeezed it straight back on and we sailed over the fence at exactly 95kt. I pulled the last of the power off while easing the yoke back, hold it off, hold it off....... and with barely a tremor the Pembroke settled gently onto the tarmac. I was very pleased, Martin appeared quite impressed and even Duncan admitted that it wasn't too bad!

Back at the parking area we ran through the pre-shutdown checks, then on Martin's "three, two, one" we both pressed and held the two roof-mounted Injector Cut Out switches to turn them off. As the props slowed to a stop, we released the ICO switches and the protracted *ppsssh* of the pneumatics was almost steam-like. As the long-drawn-out hiss shattered the sudden silence, there was absolutely no doubt that we were indeed "finished with engines". What a flight, what an aircraft!

Chapter 19
Flight Back In Time

What a morning! The stainless sky suggests some fine flying, and after an endless procession of grey, grounded days of indistinct ceilings and no sight of the sun I'm eager to get airborne. A somewhat soggy December has kept *Buzz* in the shed for longer than usual and I'm a little concerned the magnetos may have got damp, but he seems to share my enthusiasm for flight and the little engine is soon chuntering cheerfully to itself. Today I have two aims, perform a low-level aerial inspection of a WW1 Home Defence Landing Ground I'd discovered the previous week while out walking with my faithful hound, then go up to altitude to test some of the cold-weather kit my boys got me for Christmas. The cockpit seems snugger than I remember, and I ruefully admit that – along with the thermal t-shirt and long johns - I've clearly put on something else over Christmas. Taxying out I can sense *Buzz's* tiny wheels crunching across the crisp, frozen grass and note with satisfaction that the windsock is indicating a steady ten knots straight down the strip. Perfect. Throttle open and the exhausts bark out their challenge to the waiting sky. The little engine is pulling like a train, and almost as soon as I've picked the tail up the wheels skip once or twice, the wing takes the weight and we're airborne and climbing away strongly. On a hot, windless summer's day coaxing *Buzz* into flight can require a delicate touch, but today the cold, thick, oxygen-rich air is making motor, prop and wings work exceptionally well.

The location of Swinstead aerodrome is mere minutes away, and *Buzz* is soon circling above the site while I try and see if any signs of it remain. It was mostly used from 1916 to 1918 by the F.E.2b fighters of No.38 squadron, which was based at Melton Mowbray to guard against possible night raids by Zeppelins on the West Midlands. Although not a trace of any infrastructure remains, the field (and all the ones surrounding it) remain essentially unchanged, and it's not difficult to imagine a few of the biplane fighters scattered around the landing ground while fitters and riggers performed vital maintenance. A distinctly ungainly-looking aircraft, the F.E.2b was designed and built by the Royal Aircraft Factory at Farnborough. Although considered to be not as stylish or effective as aircraft produced by private companies such as Sopwith, this particular RAF design (when the Royal Flying Corps became the Royal Air Force in 1918 the aircraft factory changed its name to the Royal Aircraft Establishment) does have a minor claim to fame;- it was probably the first aircraft to be fitted with an oleo-type undercarriage which – according to Cecil Lewis – meant "it was almost impossible to make a bad landing with an F.E.2b." Lewis, who flew the type with No.23 squadron, also recalled that its water-cooled Beardmore engine featured a copper jacket, which the fitters would "polish up until you could see your face in it."

Low-level task complete, it's time for the second part of the flight, and I point *Buzz* south, towards the radiant orange orb and commence a steady climb towards Rutland Water. The giant lake looks fantastic, the surface wind has dropped and the calm, mirror-like surface is reflecting the low winter sun's golden glow, making it look almost tropical. If an F.E.2b of 38 squadron somehow fell through a hole in the space/time continuum and its crew were trying to find the field at Swinstead they'd be completely discombobulated by Rutland Water, which was only completed in 1975. Stamford, Grantham, the East Coast mainline and the Great North Road would all be where they were on their maps, but why is there a huge lake where there used to be a broad valley? As *Buzz* climbs higher and higher I huddle down behind the windscreen and wonder what life must've been like for the pilots of 38 squadron and their frail, flimsy flying machines. The wood-and-fabric construction and open cockpit would've seemed perfectly familiar, as would the absence of electronics and the sparse instrument panel, although I suspect the D.9 would've flown rings around an F.E.2b! The cold air is racing past like an icy torrent, but I'm surprisingly snug. All the extra layers (including my own!) are clearly paying off, and even though the altimeter is now showing over 5,000ft I'm feeling no discomfort at all. I've been mostly climbing into the sun (with the occasional weave to look out for Fokkers, Albatrosses and Halberstadts) and it really is most agreeable with the warmth of the sun on my face. However, as soon as I swing *Buzz* around onto a northerly heading the temperature seems to plummet. Five thousand feet in an open cockpit – in January! What was I thinking? Trim forward, throttle back and we plunge gratefully earthwards. A graceful, sweeping curve from downwind through base onto final, then roll the wings level just before we cross the hedge. There's that magic moment when the tyres seem to brush through the grass without turning, then the wheels take the weight and we're rumbling across the greensward.

The engine huffs over the last few compressions as the prop slows to a stop, but before I've even undone my harness a friendly face appears from behind the hangar door, hand outstretched. "Dave Unwin" he smiles broadly. "Really?" I reply, "what a coincidence – that's my name too". The smile fades, to be replaced by a slightly baffled expression. "No no no" he says – "you're Dave Unwin". "I know" I grin. Bob turns out to be a real aviation enthusiast and a bit of a fan, who'd been visiting relatives when he'd seen *Buzz* in the circuit. I mention that I'd been looking for the old Swinstead Aerodrome and he reveals a fascinating fact; - in 1916 No. 38 squadron was commanded by a certain Captain A. T. Harris, who later found fame as 'Butch' Harris, C-in-C Bomber Command. I wonder what he would have made of a Jodel D.9?

A few weeks later and it's the morning after the coldest night of the year so far, and the lawn is a hard, ice white. I'd been planning to fly my Jodel D.9, but these days I also have the choice of a SF-25. I do like *Buzz's* open cockpit, but it does look cold! SF-25 or D.9? I just can't decide which one to fly and consult the house oracle. "What do you think, Lizzie?" "I think you're an idiot" she replies, and two hours later, snug and warm with sunlight streaming through the big canopy and the surprisingly efficient heater toasting my toes I can only agree with her. Having enjoyed finding the old Royal Flying Corps field at Swinstead, today will be another flight back in time to one of the most dangerous periods in our nation's history, as I investigate from the air the remnants of the innocent-sounding 'Project Emily'. However, despite its rather innocuous title, Project Emily was - literally, metaphorically, and acronymically, - mad, because it was a part of what NATO called 'Mutual Assured Destruction'. In 1958 President Eisenhower and Prime Minister McMillan were concerned about the build-up of Soviet missiles and agreed to the short-term deployment of intermediate-range nuclear-armed ballistic missiles to the United Kingdom. The first Thor IRBMs were flown to Britain in Douglas C-124 Globemasters in August 1958, and eventually sixty were distributed between twenty squadrons, with each squadron controlling three missiles and based at an RAF station. One of the squadrons was based about six miles north-east of the old RFC Swinstead, at RAF Folkingham in Lincolnshire while there was another around ten miles to the south-west at RAF North Luffenham in Rutland. It's a lovely winter's day, and I'm soon orbiting over North Luffenham's bomb-cratered runways and studying the peculiar-shaped concrete bases on the east side of the airfield. Having convinced myself that they must be the remnants of the Thor pads (as I can't see what else they could be), I swing the SF-25's shapely nose onto a northerly heading. The English countryside looks calm and peaceful, but evidence of the Cold War is all around, and within minutes of leaving Luffenham evidence of the Bloodhound battery at Woolfox Lodge is sliding beneath the port wing. The 32 SAMs based here were the last line of defence for the nuclear-armed Victors and Vulcans based at nearby Cottesmore, should the Russian bombers have eluded the Lightnings launched to intercept them. Barely ten minutes after leaving Luffenham I spot Folkingham right on track. It's quite unmistakable as one of its runways is covered with dozens of scrap diggers, 'dozers and excavators. I ease the SF into a lazy orbit and yes, on the north-east side of the main runway there's two more of the same strange shapes that I saw at North Luffenham, and a third more non-descript shape - they must be the launch pads, but it looks like there was less infrastructure here. (I subsequently learn that North Luffenham was one of Project Emily's four 'Main Bases' and that Folkingham was one of its satellites).

It really is a lovely morning, and the patchwork fields look peaceful and tranquil, with few signs of life. It almost feels as if the Lincolnshire countryside is hibernating and awaiting the Spring. It's a world away from the insanity of Mutual Assured Destruction, Doctor Strangelove and the crazed ramblings of Strategic Air Command's General Thomas Power, who at one briefing memorably said, "at the end of the war, if there are two Americans and one Russian left alive, we win!" Displaying the rational pragmatism of the scientific mind, the RAND Corporation's Professor William Kaufmann irritably riposted "Well, you'd better make sure that they're a man and a woman" – causing Power to flounce out of the meeting.

That evening I did some research, and soon found myself reflecting on the vast difference between RFC Swinstead's FE2.Bs and RAF Folkingham's Thors. Barely six miles and forty years separate the two airfields, yet while an FE had a top speed of 80kt, a range of 240nm and could carry 160kg of bombs, a Thor had a top speed of almost 10,000kt, a range of 1,500nm and a 1.44 megaton thermo-nuclear warhead! (For comparison, the atomic bomb that destroyed Hiroshima was barely one-tenth of a Thor's hydrogen bomb). It seems incredible just how far the science of destruction progressed in such a short space of time, and remember, those 1.44 megatons were carried by a single missile. There would've been three based at Folkingham, and another three at North Luffenham. It's almost inconceivable, but there was the nuclear equivalent of almost ten million tons of high explosive stored at these two bases alone, and even more at nearby Cottesmore for its V-bombers. The Thors could be launched within 15 minutes of receiving the order, while the 'QRA' elements of the V-Force were expected to be airborne in the same time frame, ready, willing and able to obliterate entire cities in what would've almost certainly presaged the extinction of the human race. In 1946 Orville Wright wrote "I once thought the aeroplane would end wars. I now wonder whether the aeroplane and the atomic bomb can do it. It seems that ambitious rulers will sacrifice the lives and property of all their people to gain a little personal fame."

Now, as I sit at my desk on the first of March 2022 and listen to the terrible reports coming from Kyiv, I can't help but think that, well, I don't know what to think.

Chapter 20
Curtis-Wright Travel Air 12

"Look at that bloody windsock" I groused to Pete Brand as we approached Cromer airfield. "It's definitely favouring zero-four, but I think I'd rather take two-two's upslope." As it transpired, zero-four or two-two turned out to be the aeronautical equivalent of six and two-threes, with neither option being ideal and both leaving something to be desired!

Standing imperiously on Cromer airfield's well-kept turf two hours previously, with its bright yellow wings positively glowing in the late September sun, the immaculate Travel Air 12 completely dominated the scene. Owned by Jeremy Taylor and his son

Oliver, this big, beautiful biplane looked magnificent. It's not hard to see why Travel Airs (and especially the three-seat - 16 and 4000) are the epitome of the American barnstormer and were much favoured by the aerial nomads who plied their trade across the fields of mid-western America in the 1920s and 1930s. From the tips of the big wood propeller to the top of the curvaceous rudder, it's a very handsome machine.

While admiring the intricate metal-work of the engine (radial engines are like works of art – at least to me) it was impossible not to contemplate the tremendous history of both the aircraft and the company that had built it. The Travel Air Manufacturing Company of Wichita, Kansas was established by three future colossuses of the American aviation industry – Walter Beech, Clyde Cessna and Lloyd Stearman. Both Cessna and Stearman eventually left to establish their own companies, and by 1927 Beech was the only remaining founder member. He sold Travel Air to the Curtiss-Wright Company in 1929, but in 1932 the Great Depression caused Travel Air's closure, and the name disappeared forever.

In many respects the -12 is quite typical of American sporting aircraft of the 1920s and 30s. An unequal-span single-bay biplane, the top wing has only a small amount of positive stagger, which makes access to the front cockpit difficult.

The mainwheels are quite large, for although by 1919 Orville Wright had already written that there would be a need for "distinctly marked and carefully prepared landing places", runways were few and far between in 1929. Big wheels don't get stuck in ruts.

My overall impression was that the -12 was a rugged, robust machine which would have been well suited to the rough 'n' tumble world of the travelling barnstormer, although unsurprisingly the -16E 'Sport' was a more popular machine, being essentially the same as a -12 but with two seats in the front cockpit and powered by a 175hp Wright Whirlwind. As the old barnstormers used to say, "you can't go wrong with a Wright."

I was certainly looking forward to flying it, even though my enthusiasm was tempered slightly by the wind, or rather the lack thereof, it being 'light and variable'. Aircraft of this vintage are always flown from the back seat, and showing considerable (and – as it transpired – almost misplaced) faith in my abilities, Pete insists I take the rear cockpit, even though the front one has very few instruments and no brakes. I climb easily into the spacious rear cockpit (Pete is soon to demonstrate that access to the front is much trickier), rest my elbows on the leather-trimmed rim and survey my surroundings with considerable interest. As I'd feared, the brakes are heel-operated, but everything else seems logically located.

Fuel 'on', a couple of squirts of prime then I press the starter, count four blades and turn the magneto switch to both. A couple of cylinders catch, smoke begins to sputter from the exhaust stubs and the prop spins faster and faster. The Scarab coughs, stumbles and then catches again. The propeller dissolves into a blur, the airframe shudders and the big biplane springs to life, 90 years young. Before taking the runway, Pete encourages me to "get a feel for the brakes" as we both know I'm going to need them, so I try a few turns in both directions before following the C172 cameraship out to runway 04 in a series of very sedate S-turns. The field of view forwards is very poor - this is not an aeroplane to taxi fast!

With the few pre-flight checks complete, I taxi slowly onto the runway, roll forward a few metres to straighten the tailwheel and then slowly and smoothly (the only way to operate a radial) open the throttle. With all that metal whirling around in front I can feel that the Travel Air has a distinct preference for the left side of the runway but generous amounts of right rudder keep it rolling straight, and I quickly pick the tailwheel up, improving the field of view exponentially. With aircraft like this you know when it's ready to fly, and at about 60mph I ease back the stick, the wheels stop their restless rumbling and we slide into the sky. Pete has said that seventy is a good climb speed, and almost instantly I become aware that the Travel Air definitely isn't over-powered. It is quite a hot day and with full fuel we are very close to MAUW. The 6.9 litre radial only has 145hp with which to pull 800 very draggy kilos, and furthermore old radials like the Scarab need careful, gentle handling so as soon as we're clear of the trees I pull the power back from 2,150rpm to 1900. Obviously the relatively low wing-loading conferred by the biplane configuration does help, but all the drag produced by the interplane struts and bracing wires doesn't! An original -12Q powered by a 90-horse Gipsy can't have been much fun on a hot day, that's for sure. It's quite a thermic day so we follow the 172 cameraship out over the water for some smoother air. Biplanes are never easy to fly in formation because of the poor field of view, and this shoot was made slightly more difficult by the fact that the -12 is not exactly over-powered. However, with the pictures in the can I could relax a bit and let this wonderful old machine work its magic on me. With the engine's heartbeat pulsing through the throttle and the slipstream tugging playfully at my hair, it was a sheer delight to wheel and swing, pirouetting above the beach with the raucous BLAT! BLAT! BLAT! of the seven cylinders roaring in my ears. For a few minutes, I pull down my rose-tinted goggles, forget its foibles and let its powerful personality shine through. Gazing through the three-piece windscreen at the big round cowl, or through the sturdy wire-braced wings at the sea sparkling below really is wonderful. It's a real treat chugging up and down over the cliffs at Cromer and simply letting the experience of flying such an iconic aircraft wash over me. I get to fly a lot of different aircraft, and it is irrefutable that many modern machines often seem 'soulless'. I'm not really an animist, but have wondered if perhaps one of the reasons that a brand-new aircraft constructed from composites seems a little lifeless, is that none of its components were ever alive. The Travel Air is much more organic – it features leather and linen, yellow birch and Sitka spruce, even the flowing stylised logo on the fin would've been painted by hand. It just has so much personality and character, from the wind in the wires to the rumble of the radial. It's a real 'flight back in time' and it seems like I'm not the only one enjoying the experience; as we cross overhead the pier I can see people pointing and waving, and can't help but dream about how fantastic it would be to spend a summer barnstorming around the coast in it. Hopping rides from farmer's fields all day with my teenage sons as ground crew, sampling the local food and ale in the evening and then sleeping under the wing. What a brilliant way to spend the summer that would be! It's one of my favourite flying fantasies, but – as I was soon to discover - reality (and old aeroplanes) often have a way of bringing you back down to earth, both literally and metaphorically.

Having replaced the rose-tinted goggles with my optically-correct flight test sunglasses, I get back to work. It almost feels slightly sacrilegious to forensically examine such a venerable and historic machine, but for the sake of completeness I quickly run through the flight test card, starting with a look at the stick-free stability. This is quite strong longitudinally, very strong directionally and neutral laterally. That said, it's not yet rigged perfectly; - if you take your hands off the stick it just sits there, but if you take your feet off the pedals the slip ball does tend to migrate out to the right. I mention to Pete that I think the rudder just needs a little tweak and he replies they're already on the case. Control harmony isn't bad, although unsurprisingly the ailerons do require a firm hand as the speed builds. In the turn there is some adverse yaw, but nowhere near as much as some aircraft of this vintage. You just need a squeeze of rudder, not your whole boot. An exploration of the speed envelope was next and I note that Vne is quite low at only 120mph – but who wants to go fast in an aeroplane like this? On the other end of the speed scale the Travel Air demonstrated very benign characteristics, with plenty of aerodynamic buffet before it finally stalled and dropped the left wings at around 45mph. An ergonomic anomaly that became apparent is that with the trim at 3'o'clock and the power pulled back the trim handle and throttle lever almost interfere with each other. For a look at the cruise we chugged back along the coast with the engine loping along at a lazy 1,900rpm and the IAS eventually settled on 90mph.

While we were over the beach I'd already started to sense that the wind had developed more of an onshore flow, and as Cromer is only a couple of miles inland began to look forward to the landing with a degree of trepidation. Overhead the airfield I can clearly see that the windsock is not favouring an uphill landing and discuss it with Pete. Although I'm not overly enthusiastic about landing out of wind I favour landing downhill even less (04 has a slight dip midway and then drops off towards the railway), so with a slight sense of foreboding turn downwind for 22. On base, I pull the throttle back and start to descend. Luckily for me the -12 is quite speed-stable, and although my turn onto final and initial line-up isn't perfect, a quick prompt from Pete gets me back on track. On short final I note that the windsock is now indicating a quartering tailwind, and it suddenly occurs to me that I'm already committed to land, as something tells me a go-around isn't advisable. It's a hot day, we're heavy and this big, draggy biplane is not over-powered. Over the displaced threshold with the speed nailed to 60 I close the throttle and start easing the stick back ...back...back. All three wheels kiss the grass in a gratifyingly smooth touchdown (Pete had said the undercarriage was a flatterer), and for long seconds the Travel Air runs straight-and-true, helped along with tiny jabs of rudder. Then the airspeed bleeds away, but we're still rolling along at about 10mph and I suddenly sense that the rudder is no longer having any effect. Slowly, almost imperceptibly but inexorably, the nose starts a gentle swing to the left which I catch with a deft dab of right brake. This swings the nose back and then through our desired heading, and now it's starting to swing to the right. Then, just when I need the brake most my left boot heel skims over the top of the brake pedal and it looks like we're about to ground-loop 'off piste'!

Frantically I manage to get my heel back on the pedal and a swift sharp stab swings the nose back to the left and the lower right wing passes *over* the top of the stubble! Now we're facing up the runway again so it's right brake then both brakes and phew! We're stopped, and nothing is broken or even damaged (except my pride) but at least that's all.

Taxi back up to the clubhouse and I let the motor idle for a minute to let both its oil pressure and my blood pressure subside, then turn the mags off, the engine huffs over the last few compressions and the prop slows to a stop. It wasn't quite a groundloop but it wasn't far off. I'm mortified (in fact, I wrote this the following day and was still mortified!) It's the closest I've ever come to scratching the paint during a flight test, and although Peter and Jeremy are very good about it (I subsequently learn it has a well-deserved reputation for humbling better pilots than me, as the log books show that twice in its long history it has been seriously damaged in ground loop incidents) I am embarrassed. Note that the observations about its ground-handling are not meant as criticisms of the Curtiss – no aircraft of this vintage cares for crosswinds – and as for tailwinds....! In fact, it just wasn't the right day for flying such an iconic, idiosyncratic machine from a narrow grass strip. A wide grass field that's slap into a cool 15kt wind and I could shoot touch and goes in it all day, but a relatively narrow sloping runway on a hot day with the sea breeze coming in and the wind all over the place? No thanks - I won't make that mistake again. Ninety years ago, this aircraft taught many people to fly, and today it gave me a very valuable lesson – don't land it out-of-wind!

Chapter 21
Don't Take Chances

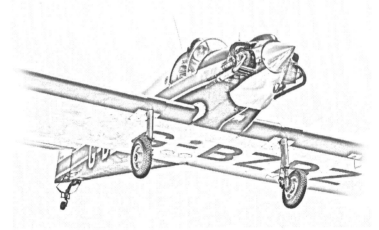

I regard the windsock with a jaundiced eye, and can't quite shake a slight feeling of disquiet. It's one of the hottest days of the year so far, and the strengthening wind is *right* across the main runway. While tugging with the EuroFox at Saltby a few days previously one of the organisers of the inter-university competition had asked if I could get the K-7 out later in the week. He was expecting a lot of students who were keen to fly, and was concerned that there might not be enough two seaters. Would I mind? Of course not! So here I am.

I look again at the windsock but the tale it tells is still the same, and all the while I procrastinate the mercury continues to rise. Indeed, the density altitude at Black Spring farm is already over 1,200ft. One of the challenges of operating from farm strips is that the accelerate-stop distance can at times barely exist and you can be committed to going quite early in the takeoff roll. At least Farmer John has mowed the grass recently and it's nice and short, but practically everything else is against us. *Buzz* is waiting patiently on the chocks with his sharp-pointed spinner pointing questioningly at the sky. I throw a clump of freshly mown grass into the air and it only confirms what I already knew. Einstein's definition of insanity was to repeat an experiment and expect a different outcome, so rather than do that I walk over to *Buzz*, check that the tail is tied down set the throttle and magnetos and decide to leave the decision with him. He's been a bit balky to start recently; if he doesn't want to go flying today he'll let me know. I gave the toothpick prop a half-hearted flip and wouldn't you know it, he roars instantly into eager life. Typical! Having given the matter careful consideration I decide to take off to the north-west, which will allow me to begin my takeoff run in a great sweeping arc across the widest part of the strip. The moment is now and I push the throttle to the stop and quickly pick up the tail to improve acceleration. The crosswind is considerable and I concentrate on keeping straight as we charge up the strip. My practised eye takes in the information from the elementary instrumentation in a single glance. The gauges are good, but although the speed across the ground is increasing the airspeed isn't and the wing seems reluctant to take the weight in the hot, thin air. Just as I'm thinking about snatching the throttle back the wheels skip. *Buzz* still isn't ready to fly though, and the far hedge is now the near hedge. With a sudden jolt of adrenaline, I realise there is no longer enough strip left to stop. The wheels skip again and *Buzz* is flying in ground effect, but I resist the temptation to climb. This is no time for anything but the finest of airmanship, and a very wise old aviator once said to me "if it looks like you're about to hit something, aim so that you *just* miss it". Suddenly the hedge is here, I apply just a couple of grams of backpressure on the stick and *Buzz* skims over the shrubbery and into the sky. We're safely airborne, the airspeed's increasing and I exhale. As the adrenalin subsides relief soon gives way to anger, and now we're climbing I am furious with myself. Good old *Buzz* – and stupid old Dave! 'Never take a chance if you don't have to' is an aviation maxim that has been quite literally written in blood. I didn't have to fly over to Saltby and could've just as easily driven, yet I deliberately and unnecessarily painted myself into a corner, and only just got away with it. Stupid.

Over at Saltby they're lining up the gliders on the active runway, which has the strengthening wind straight down the centreline. Turning final I can see there's plenty of modern two-seaters. It appears that - having stupidly risked my neck and my aircraft to get there I'm not even needed, which would serve me bloody well right. As it transpires I am needed but the K-7 isn't; - they do have plenty of two seaters but not enough tugs, so would I mind flying the DR400 instead? Of course not! Having put *Buzz* in the main hangar and transferred my kit into the cockpit of his much bigger brother I sit with my arm resting on the canopy rail and review recent events. Why did I do it? I don't know. Later the same evening I ask myself the same question, and still don't know.

All writers – and most readers, rightly hate repetition, but I will risk your ire on this occasion; - never take a chance if you don't have to.

Chapter 22
Avro XIX

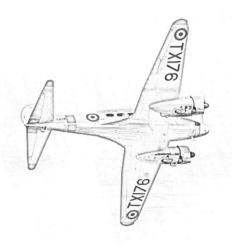

It's a warm July evening, and as I gaze down from the Anson's cockpit at Old Warden's sun-scorched strip I can't help but think it looks somewhat short after Farnborough's enormous runway. Still, I'm not stressed because I'm not doing the landing. There's practically no wind and Pete has the only brake lever on his yoke, so we've decided that I'll fly the approach down to about 50 feet, and when it's apparent that it would've worked (or not!) I'll go around and he will land it. Consequently, I'm totally relaxed, and the combination of calm conditions, excellent coaching and a stable aircraft produce a very steady approach. We sail across the hedge with the angle to the threshold, speed and sink rate all perfect, and as good landings come from good approaches, I'm confident a good landing would've resulted. "OK Dave, go around". Aware of the propensity of British interwar radials to suffer from 'rich cuts' if the power is increased too quickly, I add just enough to arrest the sink rate, pause while each engine's rpm stabilise, and then slowly and progressively open the throttles while Pete retracts the undercarriage and then the flaps. I wind on some nose-down trim, turn the Anson back onto the downwind leg and Pete looks across at me and grins. "Very nice Dave, lovely and smooth. In fact, that was such a stable approach that you may as well land it off the next one." Suddenly, I'm not quite so relaxed, but more excited than nervous. What a privilege! The Avro Anson is one of those aircraft that really is an unsung hero. It may not have the bravado of a Beaufighter, the machismo of a Mosquito, or the iconic status of its immortal stablemate the Lancaster, but the old 'Annie' performed sterling service in myriad roles with the RAF from 1936 to 1968, and was even used as a multi-engine trainer for pilots converting on to the Meteor jet fighter. In fact, the Anson, which was designed by the great Roy Chadwick, was one of the most successful aircraft ever produced by A.V. Roe and Co, with over 11,000 being built in England and Canada. It first flew in 1935, remained in production until 1952 and some were still earning their keep well into the 1970s! Airworthy Ansons are rare, and although we used 'Anson' as our callsign, it isn't. Golf Alpha Hotel Kilo X-ray is an Avro 652A Type XIX Series 2, and was built in 1946 in Avro's factory at Yeadon (now Leeds Bradford) as the Series 2 prototype. It has been owned by the BAE Systems Heritage Flight since 1981, and has been based at Old Warden with the world-famous Shuttleworth collection since 2002. It's been on display during the Farnborough airshow and now needs to be returned home on the evening of the last day. Would I be interested in being its co-pilot? What do you think? BAE Systems Heritage Flight pilot Peter Kosogorin will be my mentor and captain, and as he is on the air show's flying committee we're not going anywhere until the show ends, so I take the time for a languid pre-flight. The fuselage is a steel-tube structure that's mostly fabric-covered except for the nose section which uses plywood. The wing is mostly metal, and carries a pair of Armstrong Siddeley Cheetah supercharged seven-cylinder air-cooled radials fitted with Dowty-Rotol metal two-blade constant-speed propellers and fed from fuel tanks located outboard of the nacelles. The undercarriage appears to use sections of Armco barrier for the rear actuating struts, while the mainwheels feature pneumatic drum brakes and retract into the engine nacelles (which, curiously, are not fitted with cowl flaps). In common with some other designs of this era even when retracted about half of each wheel still protrudes, and the brakes still work. Pete arrives and promptly changes into an old flying suit. "Getting into character eh?" I observe. Pete grins good naturedly but he has the last laugh. As always with a radial the first thing to do is to pull each engine through several blades (to avoid hydraulic lock) and when we've done that and venture into the wheel-wells to open the oil shut-off valves, my shirt pays the price. Access to the cabin is via a door on the port side, just aft of the wing, and having stepped over the main spar I sit down in the co-pilot's seat and take stock. I'd assumed that a British twin engine aircraft designed in the thirties would be an ergonomic nightmare, and I'm not disappointed. It's terrible.

Starting any radial engine is part procedural, part ritual, for if it is recalcitrant, invocations are not infrequent, curses are common and prayers may be proffered! Eventually the myriad buttons, handles, knobs, levers, plungers and switches are pulled, pushed, set, turned or twisted – and we're ready to start. Although designed for single pilot operations, Pete and I are going to operate it as a crew. Indeed, simply starting it by yourself would not be easy, for while Pete presses the port engine's starter and ignition boost buttons with the fingers of one hand and guards the throttle with the other I'm equally busy with the primer (which, you may recall, is behind his seat) and the mags (which are only turned on after the engine fires). The starboard motor seems inclined towards another couple of squirts of primer to keep it running and smoke sputters from the exhaust until suddenly the remaining cylinders catch, the propeller blades morph into a single shimmering circle and the Cheetah settles into a lazy growl. Pete is a BAE Systems Test Pilot and the takeoff brief is both concise and comprehensive, and includes the procedures to be adopted in the event of an engine failure both before and after the single engine best climb speed of 80kt has been attained. We also review the other critical airspeeds, such as the limiting speeds for the undercarriage and flaps, and he reminds me that a good climb-out speed will be around 90, that full power (+4 boost and 2,550rpm) is limited to a maximum of five minutes, and that the only hydraulic pump is on the port engine. In common with similar aeroplanes of this era, the single-engine performance is far from sparkling, and if you were flying an early version by yourself, the non-feathering propellers and an undercarriage that had to be wound-up by hand meant that the only way to deal with an engine failure after takeoff would've been to slam the other throttle shut and land ahead. And although there's two of us, a hydraulic undercarriage and feathering props, if anything happens to an engine low down that's exactly what we'll do, close the other throttle and land straight ahead, and to facilitate this we intend to leave the wheels down until 'land ahead' is no longer an option. Carefully, I align the Anson with runway 24's centreline. A significant advantage is that we're some 1,200kg below the 4,717kg MAUW. Negatives are that Pete has the only brakes, and the tailwheel doesn't lock, but on the plus side the runway is wide, and there's almost no wind. I'm quietly confident that as long as I bring the power in slowly I can keep it straight without Pete helping with the brakes, and as there's 2,000m of runway in front of us I bring the power in *very* slowly, wait until the rudder starts to bite then open both throttles up to +4 boost. The Cheetah's growl turns into a roar. Check the rpms are 2,550 and the airspeed's alive, then slowly raise the tail. The combination of radial engines turning big props means there's a mass of metal whirling around on the wings, and gyroscopic precession is not to be taken lightly. Pick the tail up too quickly and a swing is almost inevitable but - and as is so often the case with taildraggers - if you're ready for the swing then it doesn't come. The airspeed continues to build, the mainwheels start to skip as the wing takes the weight and at about 60kt I ease the Anson into the air and hold it down, just above the runway. Height may be money in the bank, but speed is money in your pocket. As the speed hits 90kt landing ahead is no longer an option, and once the wheels are in the wells I bring the throttle and prop levers back to a rough approximation of +2 boost and 2,300rpm and climb onto a northerly heading. It's a glorious evening, and I soon level off, adjust power to the 'max continuous' of +1 and 2,100rpm and re-trim. Talking of trim, I only ever adjusted the elevator's, and even then no more than one turn of the wheel. The ASI soon settles on 120kt, but the thirsty Cheetahs are still drinking about 150lit/hr while I'm drinking in the experience. Gazing out along the wing, past the bulbous engine cowlings and proud RAF roundels at the English countryside is a real treat, particularly as it looks stunning in the late evening sun, and the field of view from the extensively glazed cockpit is exceptional. Once we're clear of Farnborough I start to get a 'feel' for the aircraft. A couple of turns with varying angles of bank is always a good place to start an examination of the general handling, and this soon reveals that the Anson flies like it looks, for although the controls are reasonably effective they are quite heavy. Even relatively steep 360° turns aren't difficult; the control authority is good and the controls reasonably harmonised, although the elevator does seem to have more power than the ailerons. Unsurprisingly, directional control is good (but then the rudder is huge) while from a stability perspective it is stable laterally and longitudinally, and positive directionally. I don't think it'd be too taxing to fly on instruments. Decelerating for a look at slow flight is interesting, and deafening! The undercarriage warning warn has clearly been stolen from a car, and as I reduce power and speed with the wheels 'up' it blares quite disconcertingly. With a bit of flap and a dribble of power I actually get the ASI's needle flickering just below

199

60, before barely a tremor shakes the aircraft. It's very benign. For a look at the single engine performance I ask Pete to replicate a failed engine and feathered prop by setting the power on the port engine so that I effectively have zero-thrust. We're clean (flaps and wheels up) and light (a long way below MAUW), but the density altitude of over 3,000ft makes the test valid. I can induce the Anson to climb at 85kt, but just barely. The official RAF *Pilot's Notes* which I studied assiduously before my flight, state quite clearly that "if engine failure occurs before the undercarriage is raised, it may be impossible to climb away" – and *Pilot's Notes* were usually written by men whose style was inclined to understatement. I'm quite sure that it would be impossible to climb with the wheels down after an engine failure, and that a single-engine go-around would also be extremely fraught. Pete suggests I might try a more spirited manoeuvre to see what it's like to display an Anson, so I increase power to +2 and 2,200rpm, accelerate to 140kt (Vne is 185) and then pull up into a lazy chandelle. It's fun, but it's not what an Anson is about and for the rest of the flight I elect to rumble sedately across the countryside and just soak up the ambience of flying a vintage twin on a beautiful evening. The

Cheetahs are literally purring, the light is glorious and I think that Pete is also greatly enjoying the flight as we don't even talk that much but just watch the world sliding by under our broad wings. Far too soon the giant airship sheds at Cardington appear, irrefutable evidence that our journey is nearly at an end, and we're soon sliding into the circuit at Shuttleworth. Old Warden has been hosting an aeromodellers event and as several are camping overnight they are still flying, so Pete suggests I 'make a bit of noise' to alert them that we intend to land, reiterates that I'm to go around at 50ft and reminds me that at only 85 the flap limiting speed is quite low. The windsock looks languidly limp so we elect to use 03, which will allow us to make full use of the runway extension and has the advantage (for me at least) of putting the runway on my side, as it's a right-hand circuit. As the intention is to land this time I extend slightly further downwind. Pete lowers the undercarriage first, which changes the trim slightly 'nose down' and then adds some flap, which pitches the nose back up. After a brief base leg, I settle the Anson onto final, double check that the props are set fully fine, glance at the brake triple pressure gauge and then concentrate on maintaining the correct speed and angle. The field of view is excellent, and as we sail over the fence I add a pinch of power to arrest the increasing sink rate, pause, then slowly close the throttles while gently easing the yoke back. "Don't flare too high" cautions Pete, so I hold what I have, wait until we've sunk a little, and then ease into the flare and hold off. The touchdown isn't bad at all, but weeks of drought mean the grass is like corrugated concrete, and we bounce and skip a couple of times before settling. (One of the aeromodellers later told me it looked smooth, so it probably felt worse than it was). Pete applies a couple of deft applications of brake, the Anson slows to walking pace and we park over by the gate and run through the shutdown checks. I then pull out and hold the 'Slow Running/Cut-Out handle, but just like me, it seems as if the Anson is reluctant to quit flying for the day. The Cheetahs continue growling until the fuel stops flowing and the engines slowly die away into nothingness, accompanied by the whirring diminuendo of the decelerating gyros. Finally, and with a degree of regret, I snap the big black Bakelite Ground/Flight switch to 'Ground'.

Chapter 23
Lights, Camera – Action!

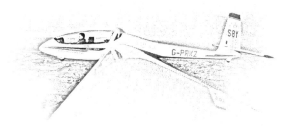

If the gliding club's CFI says, "You're wanted in makeup Dave" it is unlikely that they mean it. However, if there's a camera crew filming then they may be alluding to the fact that you need a touch more eyeliner as you're in the next scene, love! As I wrote earlier, there's no business like tow business; the roar of the engine, the smell of the crowd. It also makes for excellent television, and over the years I've flown for the cameras of the BBC, HTV, ITN, S4C and even (unlikely as it may seem) the microphones of Radio Wales!
I remember flying the Buckminster GC's Remorquer for Woodcut Media, which was filming an episode about assault gliders for

its popular series *'Defenders of the Sky: The Great British Airfield'*. However, despite flying the tug - and be definition having the 'lead' role - I wasn't the star (and don't think I won't be having a word with my agent!) Jules Hudson did a great job (its occasionally repeated on The History Channel) but during the briefing I was reminded that while filming is always interesting and good fun – it can have its moments!

As always - the first thing to be considered is the weight and balance. The weight of the camera, and the balance of the money owing. These days the cameras are so tiny that their weight isn't an issue, but sometimes the weight of the presenter is. Filming also takes a lot of time and can be noticeably wearing for people who are not used to standing around on a windy airfield unsuitably dressed. I'm not saying all media people are a bit fey, but just be careful if you have any planning restrictions about camping on the airfield. It all takes a lot of takes before the director finally says "Alright loves, it's a wrap" and I well remember one occasion when after a long series of takes on what the producer informed me was " a desperate effort to add even a hint of verisimilitude to what was undoubtedly a bald and deeply unattractive narrative" the presenter eventually became so cold and wooden that they could have used Pinocchio as his stunt double! Furthermore, the sound recording is invariably affected by wind, and there's often a lot of wind at the gliding club. However, that could be diet related, or simply due to the amount of ale consumed the night before.

All joking aside, cameras and aircraft can be a potent – and at times lethal – combination. A great many pilots have died making 'one last pass for the camera' (including Paul Mantz in *Flight of the Phoenix*), Art Schol was killed while filming *Top Gun* and several pilots died making *Hot Shots*. Neil Williams and James Gilbert had their fair share of thrills while filming *Aces High* as the demands a director may make can be pretty demanding. Would you fancy a formation takeoff downwind in an underpowered taildragger? Of course not, and I bet they didn't either.

A few years ago I greatly enjoyed flying with one of the great movie stunt pilots, Corkey Fornof. His career is more like a movie than some of the movies he's been in - and he's been in a lot of movies! Although you may not necessarily know his name - you have definitely seen him in action. Not just in Bond films such as Moonraker, License to Kill or Octopussy but also other big box-office hits, including, Face/Off, The

Phantom, and Six Days and Seven Nights. He explained just how much planning goes into a shoot, and that it's never a case of 'here, hold my beer, and watch this!'

It is irrefutable that cameras do bring out the worst in pilots (the BGA even had to issue a warning about the potential problems caused by Go-Pros and 'selfie sticks') while one of the dumbest things I ever did was while filming for a BBC feature on gliding. The cameraman was a 'character' who claimed to have covered several wars, and he managed to rev us all up to get something 'special'. Anyway, when I towed him aloft in the T-21 I emphasised that he should keep the camera trained on the Pawnee when the towrope released. Instead of breaking away I climbed straight ahead, then rolled inverted and pulled through, intending to pass directly under the T-21. Big mistake! As the ASI's needle raced towards Vne I stopped looking at it and concentrated on making as smooth a recovery as possible. Well, the tail stayed on, but it was a very chastened - and somewhat shaken - tug pilot that gingerly crept back to the airfield. I then spent the next 30 minutes carefully checking that nothing had fallen off the Pawnee while waiting for my heartbeat to subside! By all accounts it looked truly spectacular, but annoyingly we never got a copy of the footage, and it didn't make the final edit. In fact, it's been my experience that they never use the best bits. I well remember carefully explaining to camera why we called a local mountain by its Welsh name Twmpa (pronounced Tumpa) and rarely used its English name; Lord Hereford's Knob. "It is because" I leered into the lens, "most of the boys find Lord Hereford's Knob a bit of a mouthful, although some of the lady pilots can get their tongue round it."

Perhaps unsurprisingly, that bit didn't make the final cut either!

Many years later, and after having spent several days in a socially distanced studio shooting a new TV series called 'Plane Crash Recreated', I was more than happy when noted producer Daniel Sharp of SWR Media suggested sending cameraman Sammy Purcell up to Saltby to shoot some B-roll of me flying. SWR produced the acclaimed 'Disasters Engineered' TV series for the Discovery Channel, although modesty precludes me mentioning my involvement in the series, I'd be doing myself (and the crew) a disservice if I failed to mention in passing that it was nominated for an Emmy......

Of course, as we gathered outside the clubhouse in a socially distanced style the crusty old club members were all intrigued when I revealed that I'd need one of the sailplanes around lunchtime for some TV work, with several keen to offer their services as extras for the crowd scenes. "I guess there's no chance of a speaking part?" implored one fame-hungry flyer "just a line?" "Good guess" I grinned "there's no chance!" Warming to my theme, I explained that all we needed was some B-roll to supplement footage shot in the studio the week before. "Is B-roll the same as a pick-up?" asked another member. "Oh no" I replied (and trying to sound as if I knew what I was talking about while struggling to keep a straight face) "a pick-up is a small, relatively minor shot filmed or recorded after the fact to augment footage already shot. On the other hand B-roll is very different. It is supplemental or alternative footage intercut with the main shot." I could sense some of the members regarding me in a new light, so to keep the joke going I started burbling on about continuity, the techniques of 'dissolve, lap, dissolve' and flash editing, the usefulness of selective focusing and the vital importance of always carefully balancing the mise-en-scène with tight, accurate framing. There was what theatre directors call 'a pregnant pause', then one of my audience grinned and opined, "you're just talking bollocks, aren't you?" Guilty as charged" I laughed.

"Shall we get the gliders out to the runway?"

As we towed the sailplanes out the banter continued, with one of the members asking me whether I was an adherent of the 'classical' acting technique, or considered myself more of a 'method actor'. "It depends" I responded. "If we shoot some B-roll of me flying the tug, I'll probably lean more towards 'method'. "And what method is that" he enquired. "I try not to crash" I replied. "Ahh, the vagaries of tow business' quipped another, referencing a previous column of mine in Pilot magazine, "how do you do it"? "Easy" I retorted, "I am well-known as a tow business personality!" Cameraman Sammy is a keen paraglider pilot so having been allocated the SZD-54 Perkoz, our first task is to carefully mount a GoPro on the port wing. Sammy will then sit in the back of the Perkoz with another camera so that he can film the forthcoming flight from two very different perspectives, 90° apart.

It's a stunningly beautiful winter's day so we take a high tow to 4,000ft to maximize our flight time. Obviously, Sammy's here to do a job, but if there's time I'd also like to show him just how well a modern two-seat sailplane performs. First, we must shoot some footage, so under Sammy's direction I carefully manoeuvre the Perkoz to make the best advantage of the sun, bearing in mind we're shooting with two cameras at right angles to each other. It's not easy but good fun and interesting. Eventually Sammy says he's got loads of footage so I urge him to put the camera down and get on the controls. He proves to be an eager and able pupil and although he has no three-axis experience he does have 'the touch' and we're both very pleased at the progress he's making as we slide through a sublime sky. Just before I resume control prior to joining the circuit Sammy performs a near-perfect three-sixty. We're both well chuffed.

Back on the ground he takes a quick look at the 'rushes' and is happy, but as with all the photographers and cameramen I've worked with he wants more, so I suggest we use the K-7 for some winch-launch footage. This we do, and – as I'd expected – the 0-60 in three seconds and 2,000ft/min climb rate get his full attention – and approval! He then spends the next couple of hours shooting random pick-up shots of me hooking on the winch cable, signalling the tug, running the wing and various other launch point-related activities. Initially I'm a bit self-conscious (as I know the watching members are just dying to rip the piss) but soon forget I'm being filmed and just get on with launching the gliders. And I do get my proverbial revenge when someone walks over to ask a perfectly legitimate question and I cut him off with an abrupt "sorry, no autographs. Can't you see I'm working?" Finally, I get the chance to put Sammy in the tug and we shoot yet more footage during a high tow, including some extremely steep turns during the descent. He seems very happy with how the day has gone, and as we pull up outside the hangar and shut the engine down I can't help but ask "is this where you say, 'alright love, that's a wrap'?" "I very much doubt it" he replied. It has been a fun day with plenty of flying in three different types, so you may imagine my delight when – a few days later – I receive an email from ace film editor Matt King, directing me to a GoogleDrive file. Here I find a glorious pastiche of Top Gun, complete with Harold Faltermeyer's iconic score and Steve Stevens scorching guitar. For complicated copyright reasons, it could not be shared on social media, but trust me, its brilliant. Lizzie almost wet herself laughing when she saw it!

Chapter 24
Pilatus PC-21

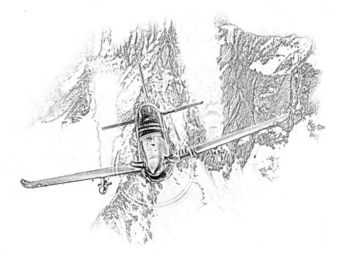

The iconic north face of the Eiger looms large as we flash past just below the summit. I roll into a tight, four 'g' turn, lower the nose and slalom back down through the snow-covered alpine valleys at just over 300kt. This is just *way* too much fun and as we scorch over a glacier, turn towards a lake and start lining a bridge up in the gunsight for a rocket attack I can't help but think that – although this aircraft can be used as a weapon, it would make a great toy!

The day had started at the Pilatus factory in Stans, Switzerland, where I met ex-

Luftwaffe Tornado pilot Martin 'Canyon' Mendel and then headed off to the equipment section to be measured and fitted with a helmet and the rest of my flying kit. The technician takes one look at me and says I need one of the g-suits that are usually reserved for visiting generals (and no, these are not particularly luxurious g-suits, just slightly larger than average ones!) Once issued with all my equipment it's time for the mission briefing. Just as it is on an operational squadron, every sortie is fastidiously planned, right down to the minute when we walk out to the aircraft. There's an enormous amount of information to assimilate and an incredible number of acronyms and initialisms! This is SOP, as it allows the maximum amount of info to be communicated ASAP ie PDQ – QED! Briefing complete, I squeeze into my g-suit. It's been eight years since I last wore a pair of 'speed jeans' and it shows as I wrestle with the myriad zips, fasteners, Velcro strips and press studs. Once suitably attired, I waddle out to our waiting aircraft with a certain amount of excited anticipation. Approaching the PC-21 I am struck by just how attractive it is. The 'Ferrari Red' paint scheme really suits it, while the colour and lack of weapons make it look like a high-end sport plane, not a weapon of war. As we begin to move around the aircraft, I note that the trailing-link undercarriage looks particularly robust, while the myriad access panels suggest servicing should be relatively straightforward. Canyon confirmed that the aircraft has proven to be very reliable in service and that it's "just like a Swiss watch. Beautifully made and very dependable." Some of this dependability clearly comes from its Pratt & Whitney PT6-68B, which turns a five-blade composite prop. Although the engine's maximum power output is 1,600shp, this is scheduled as a function of airspeed through the Power Management System (PMS). Consequently, at speeds below 80kt even bending the throttle (it's actually called the PCL or power control lever, as it also controls the propeller) over the stop won't give you more than 1,080shp, while the full 1,600 isn't available until 200kt has been attained. It's a very clever system, which greatly reduces rudder inputs during take-off, and it's this combination of the PMS and automatic yaw compensation provided by the TAD (Trim Aid Device) that allows the -21 to more accurately replicate the characteristics of a jet. The wing is also interesting, as the leading edge is slightly swept back, while lateral control is provided by both ailerons and spoilers.

Having climbed up to the rear cockpit, I settle myself into the Martin-Baker Mk16 zero-zero ejection seat and begin the process of strapping in and connecting myself to the aircraft. It is important this is done correctly, as you become an integral part of the aircraft and can only move your head, arms and legs. The various display screens suddenly illuminate as Canyon begins to bring our PC-21 to life. I lower my clear visor and confirm I have done so over the intercom, allowing Canyon to lower and lock the canopy. It is imperative your visor is down before the canopy is shut, in case the miniature detonating cord (MDC) malfunctions and shatters the canopy. Interestingly, only the front part of the canopy is fitted with MDC as it is bird-strike proof up to 300kt. I then remove the safety pin from the ejection seat, and reflect that as I'm now sitting on a live rocket it's best to keep my hands clear of the firing handle. Starting the engine is turbine-simple – just press the 'start' button and, above 13% turbine rpm (Ng), move the PCL out of its detent and into idle. We get a nice cool start, with the gauges indicating well below the maximum allowable temperature. While Canyon continues with the post-start checks, I familiarise myself with the cockpit layout, controls and instrument panel The HOTAS system features 14 different buttons and switches and some have more than one function! All the primary flight and navigation information is displayed on the HUD and the rear cockpit HUD repeater, along with the weapons aiming data. The panel is dominated by a central primary flight display (PFD) and two large MFDs; there are no analogue standby flight instruments except a 'Whiskey' compass, and even that is probably superfluous – the secondary flight display (SFD) has its own battery, and more than enough info to get you home. Having scrolled through the useful electronic checklist Canyon sets up the MFDs so that I have the moving map on the left and engine performance data on the right, and we taxi out. Once we're across the road that separates the factory from the airfield (having waited dutifully for a green traffic light) Canyon hands control to me. The PC-21 is an easy aircraft to taxi, with a fine field of view (the rear seat is stepped-up slightly), positive nosewheel steering through the rudder pedals and powerful, progressive brakes. With the flaps set to take off, I roll out onto the runway, line up with the centreline and bring the power up to 40% against the brakes. The PC-21 squats down on its nosewheel like a sprinter on the blocks, a final check of the engine performance data and I release the brakes and simultaneously push the PCL up to the stop. A sudden jerk and we bound forward and race down the runway. As advertised, and very impressively, despite the fact the engine is already putting out 1,080shp only a small amount of right rudder is required to track the centreline. The airspeed comes alive and the speed starts building at a gratifyingly fast rate. I rotate slightly early but the acceleration is such that it isn't an issue. As we race into the sky with both speed and power continuing to increase I quickly raise the undercarriage and flaps and climb away with the speed building past 200kt and all 1,600 horses pulling eagerly. Within seconds I can tell this is my sort of aircraft. The handling is really crisp and precise, the field of view exceptional and there's plenty of power. It also really does feel like a jet, as the speed, lack of vibration and rock-solid ride make it unlike any prop-driven aircraft I've ever flown. As the wing is quite small, the wing-loading is relatively high and it slices through some light, choppy turbulence as if it wasn't there. The PC-21 is definitely an aircraft that flies through the air, not upon it. Although Canyon had emphasised that it really does possess similar qualities to a modern jet trainer, I'm still surprised and impressed by just how 'jet-like' it is. Indeed, apart from the prop, the biggest clue that we aren't in a jet is that the fuel flow gauge shows we're only burning about of 200kg of Avtur an hour. The pressurisation system works so smoothly I don't even notice the prodigious rate of climb.

Canyon encourages me to 'wring it out' and a few steep turns and sharp reversals confirm that the handling is every bit as good as I'd been told it was – and my ability to handle 'g' has not diminished with age. Canyon then takes control, selects air to ground mode, and attacks a bridge with virtual bombs. Just as if we were on the range dropping practice bombs we get a near instantaneous score (20m at 4.30- good job Canyon!) but, with just a couple of keystrokes, the bombs reappear on the stores management page allowing me to have a go. Today, all our weapons are virtual, but the PC-21 has one centreline and four underwing hardpoints that allow it to carry up to 1,150kg of air-to-ground weapons or ferry tanks. Canyon also demonstrates the synthetic radar and RWR panel as we flash past virtual SAM and gun sites on our mission through the mountains. Flying at low level and 300kt through the Alps is tremendously exciting. It also gives me the chance to sample the fine handling as Canyon says: "OK hard right at the next mountain, then reverse and turn left down the valley towards that lake." Canyon sets us up for a rocket attack on another bridge and then demonstrates a toss-bomb attack on a nearby airfield. Once again, we get near instantaneous scores; with the MFD showing that the rockets went slightly long, but the bomb was a direct hit. I try my hand at rocketry (with mixed results!) before we climb swiftly up to 10,000ft for some aerobatics, spins and stalls. Aileron rolls are easy - the combination of ailerons and spoilers for lateral control gives the PC-21 a roll-rate of around 210°/second - but my four-point hesitation roll leaves something to be desired. Loops are also perfectly straightforward – accelerate to 270kt and then pull up at a steady four g for a nice round loop. Incidentally, at the top of a loop is one of the few times when it doesn't fly like a jet, as the slow airspeed and high power setting at the apex requires just a squeeze of right rudder to keep the ball centred. After I've finished my rather rusty aerobatic repertoire with a couple of Immelmanns and a passable cloverleaf, I try a couple of stalls and it's interesting to note that the aircraft can be held in a fully-stalled attitude with quite heavy buffet, yet still retain adequate lateral control. Canyon takes control and demonstrates a six-turn spin to the left. I like how the PC-21 behaves in a spin; the nose is pitched down nicely, the rate of rotation steady and not too rapid, and recovery is both easy and immediate. Having climbed back up to 10,000ft -with a best rate of climb of around 4,000fpm it doesn't take long - I try a six-turn spin to the right. Thousands of feet below the sharply pointed nose, Lake Lucerne whirls wildly as we spin earthward. The altimeter unwinds at a prodigious rate, and we're already below the summit of many of the Alps. As the nose flicks round for a sixth time, I apply full opposite rudder and then ease the stick just forward of neutral. The spin stops almost instantly and I pull up out of the ensuing dive, increase power and soar effortlessly upward into the perfect blue of an Alpine sky. This really is a fine-handling aeroplane!

Canyon then takes over, sets the power to simulate a failed engine with feathered prop and glides back to Stans from 8,000ft. The PC-21 has a glide ratio of about 12:1, and drops 1,000ft every two nautical miles. Canyon does an excellent job of judging the glide, even though his approach is compromised by a PC-6 dropping parachutists which isn't where it's reported to be. After a touch-and-go he gives control to me and talks me round a right-hand circuit onto runway 07. Canyon is an excellent instructor and by giving me good cues on how much power to use, and when to drop the undercarriage and flaps, it all goes rather well. Although initially it seems to me that the flap selector would be better placed slightly further forward, I soon get used to it. About 120kt on base leg with undercarriage down and T/O flap works well, with a Vref of 104 and full flap. A near-perfect approach is spoilt by me holding off a metre too high, but the trailing-link undercarriage soaks it up with aplomb. Off again for a left-hand circuit; this proves to be interesting as you completely lose sight of the airfield on the downwind leg due to a large mountain being in the way! This time I've got my eye in and, although the view from the backseat isn't perfect (you do lose a bit of the picture on short final due to the HUD repeater), as we flash over the numbers I raise the nose, squeeze the PCL closed and just let it settle. I get a really nice landing which I convert into a touch-and-go, Canyon demonstrates a turn-back and we're all done for the day. What a great handling aeroplane! As we taxi back across the road I note we've barely used half of our 542kg of fuel in over an hour of flight time, most of which was done at high power settings. Back in the briefing room, Canyon downloads all the information from the Mission Data Recorder. This is an incredibly powerful debriefing tool because it completely removes any ambiguities, arguments or misunderstandings between student and instructor. It is also extremely impressive.

The next morning the weather is not good, but after lunch it looks fractionally brighter and Canyon decides to give it a try. Time is of the essence and I manage to wedge into my g-suit and strap in a lot quicker than the day before. Although I'd hoped to fly from the front, the low ceiling means that an instrument let-down is almost inevitable and my instrument flying skills are more than a little rusty. Consequently, when Canyon somewhat apologetically indicates that he'd rather sit in the front I just grin and reply I'd rather he sit in the front too! The acrid tang of jet fuel wafts across the ramp as Moritz cranks up another PC-21 and within minutes our two-ship is scorching skyward through a big blue hole and on its way to 17,000ft. Once at altitude we start off with some graceful formation 'lazy-eights' and I note how smart the other PC-21 looks. Its bright red paint scheme really stands out against the pristine white cloud and snow covered mountains. We both then turn outboard for ten miles and then back in. "Fight's on," says Canyon. But by the time I've started to decipher some of the hieroglyphics on the HUD he's already 'locked up' our opponent with our synthetic radar and called 'Fox 3'. Scant seconds later the MFD confirms that our virtual AIM-120 has destroyed the target. I try my hand at firing our various missiles and, although Moritz is clearly not trying terribly hard to avoid being shot down, I still struggle to engage our opponent efficiently. Operating the HOTAS well is simply not a skill that can be learned in one session. Switching to guns gives me a weapon even I can understand and I turn into Moritz, put the pipper on his canopy, and pull the trigger. (During the de-brief the Mission Data Recorder reveals that I fired 95 virtual rounds with good ranging, of which 6-9 had good tracking for a definite kill. It doesn't reveal that Moritz wasn't trying very hard!) As with the synthetic bomb and rocket attacks of the previous day, our dogfights are so realistic that I wonder whether piping the *'brrrpt'* of the cannon being fired and the *'whoosh'* of missiles being launched through the intercom wouldn't enhance the realism still further. At the conclusion of our air-to-air session we separate and descend into cloud. I try my hand at some instrument flying, and am relieved to find that I'm not as rusty as I'd thought, and impressed to discover that, for an aircraft with a 210° per second roll-rate, the PC-21 is a pretty good instrument platform. Nevertheless we are, quite literally, surrounded by big mountains and Canyon takes over and flies a perfect let-down, until we break-out at 100ft above MDA and directly above a large lake. We've still got lots of fuel (possibly the biggest advantage of using a turboprop instead of a jet) so we revert back to A/G mode and attack various targets, including using the synthetic radar for a bomb attack against our home airfield. It's been another great flight and is topped off with Canyon allowing me to provide, (if I say so myself) a very smooth landing. I brake hard, the anti-skid system works well, and we're stopped after quite a short ground roll. I think even Canyon might've been slightly impressed!

Chapter 25
Carry On Living Day

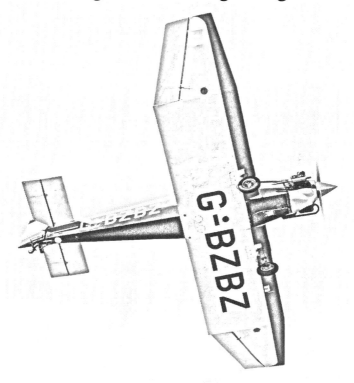

It's late in the evening on 4 August, and as I float 4,500ft above the Vale of Belvoir in my trusty Jodel D.9 *Buzz* I am profoundly content. In the Unwin household 4 August is an official Public Holiday because it's known as 'Carry On Living Day'. Today marks the second anniversary of Eskil

Amdal and I surviving our little adventure in the Sea Fury *Invincible*, and NS&I have got the day off to an excellent start with an email notification of a Premium Bond win that's enough to fill *Buzz's* tiny tank! Having exchanged cheery text messages with Eskil ("how's yer back mate?" is a popular theme) I was quietly contemplating the insides of my eyelids when I heard lots of jet noise and obviously went outside, to see a Grob Tutor flying straight towards the house at 500ft, flanked by two Typhoons. At 1100 exactly the formation passed directly over my head and the Typhoons turned into each other, reversed, did opposing 360-degree turns and headed back the way they'd come. It looked and sounded great! Of course, it was not in my honour;- merely a 'cosmic coincidence' but honestly Gentle Reader, it was just SO perfect! Speed, height, heading, timing of the break. If it had been arranged by a mate it - literally - could not have been any more impeccable with regard to my house. It really was quite remarkable.

The day turned into a glorious summer evening, and I just had to fly, but up at the strip *Buzz* is surprisingly balky to start. For a variety of reasons, I have rather neglected him of late, but can a machine truly be petulant? Finally, I look him straight in the spinner and say "Listen *Buzz*, it's a beautiful evening. Do you want to go flying or not?" One more flip of the prop and *vroom*! Of course he wants to go flying! Ten minutes later and we're racing down the strip. The normally slightly-soft surface is like concrete and having got over his fit of pique *Buzz* is pulling like a little locomotive and accelerates into the ten-knot breeze with real purpose. I don't think I've ever cleared the far hedge with a wider margin. As the wind is from the north I make the first leg of the flight directly into wind and head off up the East Coast Main Line towards Grantham. A solid surge of lift tells me there's still life in the air yet, and as the last thermal of the day oozes out of a wood and boosts *Buzz's* already surprisingly good climb rate it reminds me to make slight diversion to see what's happening at Saltby. I spot the K-21 making the last landing of the day as the Thursday evening group pack up, then carry on north towards Belvoir Castle. The farming around here is mostly arable and far below me I can see numerous combine harvesters and tractors scurrying hither and thither as the farmers metaphorically (I know it's actually grain) 'make hay while the sun shines'. Usually I assess each field's suitability in case of an emergency, but today practically every one has been harvested, and the few that haven't soon will be. It's a glider pilot's dream - virtually every field is useable, and the dust produced by the myriad machines provide an excellent indicator of the surface wind's strength and direction.

I continue climbing with the intention of going above the diaphanous clouds, but soon realise that they're higher than I thought. I also remind myself that it's sunset soon, and that although at 5,000ft I'm bathed in bright sunlight, far below shadows are already stealing silently and stealthily across the ground.

A waxing crescent moon has appeared, but it's the earth that's got my attention. Last month was the driest July for almost ninety years, and the hottest on record. Lincolnshire looks as thirsty as I feel ('Carry On Living Day' is traditionally celebrated with beer, and it's about time I had one) so I roll *Buzz* up onto a wingtip, let the nose drop and begin the long slide back to the strip. Open-cockpit flying is a very visceral experience, and along with the sights, sounds and smells, even the temperature is constantly changing. I'd always intended to climb quite high and had dressed accordingly. Consequently, I was soon overheating while taxying out, but as I climbed and the temperature dropped I'd gone from too hot, to just right to too cold. Now the reverse occurs, as the air temperature goes from too cold to just right, and with loads of height to burn off we slalom down an imaginary slope on our way to the strip. The warm air flowing past the windscreen feels wonderful, and *Buzz* seems to be enjoying it too, as the long, fast (for a D.9) dive allows him to stretch his wings. As we descend it seems like the sun is racing us to see who can reach the ground first, and I'm momentarily baffled when – in the fading light – I can't see the strip. Ordinarily it stands out well, a lush green stripe in a sea of beige, but it's been burned to almost brown-black this summer and just doesn't look the same at all. It doesn't feel the same either, and despite a nice smooth landing the combination of the super-hard surface and a very simple undercarriage gives my back a little reminder as to why I celebrate 4 August!

Printed in Great Britain
by Amazon